FROM
DARKNESS
TO
LIGHT

FROM DARKNESS TO LIGHT

The Marty Bardine Story

WHAT GOD WILL DO FOR YOU

MARTY BARDINE

XULON PRESS

Xulon Press
2301 Lucien Way #415
Maitland, FL 32751
407.339.4217
www.xulonpress.com

Paperback ISBN-13: 978-1-6322-1249-8
Ebook ISBN-13: 978-1-6322-1250-4

Table of Contents

Chapter 1

Isaiah 61:1, 3
(speaking of Jesus to come)

"The spirit of the Lord is upon me, because the Lord has appointed me to preach good tidings to the poor; He has sent Me to heal the broken hearted, to proclaim liberty to the captives, and opening to the prison to those who are bound;

To proclaim the acceptable year of the Lord, and the day of vengeance of our God; to comfort all who mourn, to console those who mourn in Zion, to give them beauty for ashes, the oil of joy for mourning, the garment of praise for the spirit of heaviness, the planting of the Lord that He may be glorified."

Good news!

Did you know that God has a plan and purpose for your life? God in his vast wisdom made everybody on the earth with a plan and purpose that will satisfy the hungry soul. Your life is not a mistake or a random existence with no real goal.

But in order to follow that purpose and goal that you are suited for, what God has designed you for, both with the gifts and talents, you must enter into a relationship with him through a covenant.

This covenant is what you must enter into in order to get God's help and blessing and wisdom and protection. And His daily care to go beyond for you what you could neither ask nor think. To get your prayers answered and to get His help in time of need and low times in your life. To lift you up when you are down is to enter into a covenant with Him.

Do not think, well I'm down here and God is up there. Poor me why can't God do me a favor once in a while? The truth is He longs to help you. But is He your God or is something else in the world your God? When you have trouble in your life and call to Him, do you seek Him out? Or do you just want to get your problem solved? If God was motivated by people's problems only, nobody would have any. Problems are an incentive to seek God out.

But God seeks faith in Jesus. This is why many go to a man of God, who walks with God, Pastor or Evangelist and then can get their problem solved. God is then glorified. He wants glory and relationship from us. Your troubles should be a motivator to seek God out until you find Him. He is never far. We have His word. If you seek out God, God will lead you to Jesus. He is the door to God.

How many times have you seen a christian tv show or heard a radio program preaching Jesus and shut it off. Maybe heard some one talking about Jesus and you walked away, wanting nothing to do with it, but yet when your in trouble you pray to God. It doesnt make sence. Yet God is merciful. He is patient. He wants you to call out to Him. He waits for you to listen to His message, believe, and recieve His Son Jesus, so He can enter your life by your permission. make you whole, body, mind and spirit. Then He is glorified in you as you see what He does for you.

Others get mad at God and then hate Him and harden their hearts towards Him. All they would have had to do is be hungry for Him, seek Him out, and read His word, and they would have found Him. He will come to you. He is no respecter of persons. His Spirit came to me at my house when I got saved.

Repetance and Jesus come first before a Holy God can live in you. Jesus blood cleanses the temple, aka, our bodys. Once the blood has been applied by Jesus being recieved by you, then a holy God who cannot touch sin will dwell in you. You will then start to see God move in your life and answer your prayers.

What does entering a covenant mean and how do we do that? By us receiving the promise, His Son Jesus Christ. Not just believing He is the Christ or acknowledging God and his existence. It is not a mental exercise. But believing and receiving His son whom He sent for our redemption. This gives us a relationship with the Father again that we are not born with, because of the fall of man in the garden of Eden. We are born under a curse. Jesus removes it.

Why do you need a relationship with God through Jesus? Because without Him you are not going to heaven! You might think, "I doing okay; I don't need Jesus and a relationship with God." That attitude will leave you vulnerable to Satan and his demons. Satan's demons are the torturers of man with sickness, disease, hopelessness, and depression. You will remain unprotected from them as long as you don't belong to Jesus. This is why so many of you have empty, miserable, joyless, lives and don't know why, and many afflictions, both mental and physical. Satan's greatest weapon is stealth. He doesn't want you to believe he exists.

Then you won't run to Jesus and put up a fight. He is defeated through your relationship with Christ. He is deathly afraid of you finding out who you really are when you are joined to Christ. You cannot be defeated. We are made in Gods image.

As you read this book you will see that I have been physically attacked by demons. I have seen them; they have attacked me in my sleep where I saw them on three different occasions. I have heard them many times audibly. They have pounded on my walls.

Attacked my flesh with a physical infirmity. I have gotten the victory every time. They disappear when I use the God's word and the name of Jesus against them. I have used the authority of the word to get my unsaved dad off of his death bed three times. Others praying also. Fear and death trying to kill him. He told me that a spirit came into his bed room one day.

It looked like the grim reaper. It was a skeleton with a hood covering his head. My dad saw it physically. He said to it, "You aren't going to get me!" He swung his arm through it, and it disappeared. He told me this story, and I knew it was the spirit of death he saw. My dad was having serious health issues later in life. He was in emergency care and in intensive care on three different occasions. I took authority over the spirit of death at all three different times, and he came out of his condition shortly. Also called others to pray who were believers. The doctors wanted him to get his last rites. Satan is afraid of us covenanting with Jesus and getting the authority that Jesus will give us as children of God to defeat him and the sin in us. God is all life, Satan is all death.

Matthew 15:18, 20

Jesus said," but those things which that proceed out of the mouth come from the heart and defile a man. Out of the heart proceed evil thoughts, and murders, adultery, fornications, thefts, false witness, blasphemies." our words.

Galatians 5: 19, 21

"Now the works of the flesh are evident which are adultery, fornication, uncleanness, lewdness, idolatry, sorcery, hatred, contentions, jealousies, out bursts of wrath, selfish ambitions, dissensions, heresies, envy, murder, drunkenness. Revelries-drunken party's; and the like of which I tell you beforehand just as I also told you in time past, that those who practice such things will not inherit the kingdom of God." Youre not going to heaven!

This is the cursed life. It is evil! This keeps you from God and getting prayers answered.All these sins listed above are satanic in nature. This is what Satan is like. Satan is cursed! He is God's enemy! We call such behavior normal because everybody does it.

When the scripture says "works of the flesh" Our flesh outer man, is an impetuous child living by the sences. Taste, smell touch, hear, see. It has evil desires, It wants what it wants now! This must be brought under the control of Jesus and He will eliminate the desires and give you self control by His Holy Spirit. This is why you see adults acting like childeren. They have not been renewed. Jesus will put these desires and habits to death if you will follow His leadings. Then you are free.

Why is sin so bad for us? It is the agreement between mankind and Satan. Satan is condemned. He will burn in the Lake of fire forever. Worms will eat him. Anyone who chooses to keep sin and not put it under the blood of christ and His offer to pay for it for you, if you will give Him your life, will suffer the same fate. You will be tortured eternally, burned, eaten by worms, tormented by demons. Darkness, no water, no hope of getting out of the lake of fire.

The difference between hell and the lake of fire is that hell is the place that people go to today if they die without christ. When a person is arrested and indicted with crimes, he or she is held in a local jail, or a temperary place until court begins and evidence is presented.

If the person is convicted and found guilty by the jury, then the judge must give the sentence according to the State or federal laws. It doesnt matter if the judge feels sorry for the convict, he must do his job and hand out the sentence according to law, casting feeling to the side. Then the convict is taken to prison, not jail where he will carry out the years of the sentence.

The lake of fire is where the person without Christ will be sent to carry out their eternal sentance. The books will be opened and read about that persons life. The criminal will know why they are going to eternal damnation. Jesus will look into the Book of life and see if they are written in it. if not, the person is sent to their eternal punishment. [Revelation 13:8 and 20:15]. It will break Jesus heart to do so because Jesus died for that person and the person refused it. But Jesus must judge sin to iliminate all the works of Satan. He must put the pain of it, to Him, to the side to judge righteously.

It will be the fulfillment of your life long desire that you had on Earth to have a life without God in it. The sin that you loved to do on the earth will be incorperated into your torture in Hell. It will be the fruit of your doings on Earth and the reward for them. {Isaiah 14:11 and 66:24], {Mark 9:48][Matthew 10:28].

I personally have met 2 people who have seen hell and lived to tell about it.

A christian gets the fruit of their doings that they did on earth, in Heaven. Rewards. A rebell unbeliever also gets the fruit of their doings in hell. God is just. He must judge sin. Earth is where we get ourselves ready for where our eternal home will be. Will yours be Heaven or hell?

But what does God say through His angels and a Heavenly host when Jesus was born in the manger?

[Luke 2:14] "Glory to God in the highest, and on earth peace, good will toward men." You hear this at christmas but what does it mean?

Gods hand of fellowship is extended out to you by sending Jesus. Jesus is the good will Son of God . Those who recieve Him get His Peace. Those who reject Gods hand of friendship will have no peace but torment. The heart of the Lord is mercy. He is reaching out to you even now to save you if you are willing and humble yourself.

This is what Jesus came to rescue us from. These sins will not be allowed in heaven. We do these things naturally because of the fall of Adam and Eve in the garden. It has gone into the seed of mankind. Everything produces after its own kind. A deer produces a deer, an oak tree produces an oak tree, and sinful man produces sinful man.

You can put a stop to it in your own personal life! God made it simple by giving us His Son Jesus to receive. By believing in Jesus and receiving Him into your heart, God then declares you righteous in His sight. Because Gods Son Jesus is righteous, He then will declare you righteous, as you receive His Son. Your own self righteousness that you developed over the years of your life will fail. It is based in pride. What seems good to you. God does not accept it! He only will accept the recieving of His Son and His righteousness.

[First John 5:18] says, We know that whoever is born of God does not sin; be he who has been born of God keeps himself, and the wicked one does not touch him." "This scripture tells us that if we put away sin under Christ, the tempter, and torturers, Satan and his demons cannot touch us, but we must put away sin or they will have legal right to afflict us.

This means since you received Christ, as you obey Him this will keep the devil from destroying your life any more, and stop you yourself from making bad decisions that also destroy your life. In [Ephesians 6: 10,16] God gives us believers our armor and our weapons to defeat the enemy. [6:12 says] "For we do not wrestle against flesh and blood, aka, people, but against pricipalities, against powers, against rulers of darkness of this age, against spiritual hosts of wickedness in the heavenly places." These spirits influence people to do evil.

1st John 5:9, 12

> "If we receive the witness of men the witness of God is greater; for this is the witness of God, which He has testified of His Son. He who believes in the Son of God, has the witness in himself; he who does not believe God has made Him a liar, because he has not believed the testimony that God has given of His Son. And this is the testimony; that God has given us eternal life, and this life is in His Son. He

who has the Son has life; he who does not have the
Son does not have life."

A demonic being can enter into a flesh person through an open
door in the spirit, through sin. Demons enter people a lot and
oppress them with evil thoughts, so they can make a door way into
your mortal body and carry out their evil desires. They can get into
your spirit, if you're not saved, and possess the person.

Evil spirits;

There is a spirit of bondage, a spirit of fear, seducing spirits,
a spirit of infirmity, a spirit of heaviness, a deaf and dumb spirit,
a spirit of jealousy, a lying spirit, a perverse spirit, a spirit of div-
ination, a spirit of poverty, a spirit of antichrist, a spirit of death,
a spirit of haghtiness aka proud and arrogant. You can feel them
when they get on you. We think its just us but these demons get in
at oppertune times. We are our own worst enemy. Run to Christ
and be delivered.

When you ask Jesus into your heart by your free will, you are
giving Jesus an open door into your heart or spirit. Same thing. He
is spirit. The Holy Spirit will then enter you by your permission and
stay with you and this will impart to you eternal life. He will begin
to deliver you of what evil you have let into your life. You will see
the difference and know without a doubt. When you receive Jesus,
it is an act of faith. Faith pleases God.

John 14:23

Jesus answered and said to him, "if anyone loves Me he will
keep my word; and my Father will love him, and we will come to
him and make our home with him."

As you can see, in order to get the supernatural workings of
God in your life, you must receive His Son. They move together

8

as one. You cannot receive God and not Jesus. You are not able to receive God without Jesus.

John 14:21, 23

"He who has My commandments and keeps them, it is he who loves me. And he who loves Me will be loved by my Father, and I will love him and manifest Myself to him." Judas not Iscariot said to Him, "Lord how is it that you will manifest yourself to us, and not to the world?

Jesus answered and said to him, "if any one loves Me, he will keep my word; and my Father will love him, and we will come to him and make our home with him.

So what happens when you receive Christ?

God gave us marriage as an example to look at.

A man and a woman meet each other and begin to date. As time goes on, they grow closer. They like each other's company. They can see that they can get along and enjoy each other despite the little differences they might have.

But up to this point if either wanted to drop out of the relationship, they could. Why? Because there is no legal obligation to each other. No commitment promised, no future plans.

Making of the covenant, legal agreement.

The man being the initiator will approach her with a proposal of marriage. If she says yes, aka, permission, he will give her a token of engagement. The ring. Now their relationship has entered a new level. They are telling the world that they are no longer in the market. They are committed to each other only.

Then the plans start for the wedding. There is a new level of expectation from each other they never had before. They plan together their big day. The woman usually works on all the details of the big day. She wants her day perfect. She will approach her fiancé for anything she will need to make the preparations. Money, or muscle. He will give her whatever she needs because of the joy that he will have a partner in life that loves him as he loves her.

The groom is proud of his wife and brings her to meet his parents. The parents will love her because she loves their son. They all develop a relationship through the son.

Their relationship is also based on strengths and weaknesses. They both have strengths to bring to the table. But they both have weaknesses. The man should be a man, and a woman should be a woman, neither stepping into the other's role.

They need each other in order to complete a good life ready to raise kids in balance.

In the marriage they will learn to work together and give a little and take a little, meshing together as one unit. Her enemies are now his enemies. And his enemies are now her enemies.

By recieving Jesus now, we are getting to know Him like this couple before we meet Him face to face. Learning to mesh with Jesus by sharing Jesus Holy Spirit in us. We will then know Him when we see Him. We begin to think the same ways. His character now becomes our character. We still all have our own individual personalitys but now we have a new heart that will not harm another person but loves them and a heart that honors God. We will not disrupt Heavens peace and joy.

So what happens when we receive Jesus?

God and Jesus make a covenant. A legal agreement with us. [Genesis 15: 7,18]

So Jesus then offers us Himself, to make a covenant with us. He is the initiator. First John 4:19 says," We love him because he first loved us."

Jesus is called the second Adam. We the believers are the second Eve. The bride of Christ. Both loyal to God. Satan is then kicked out of the Earth forever and destroyed along with his demons and human followers. The first Adam committed high treason, he rebelled against Gods command. Eve was decieved, disobeying her husband Adam. Eve was not there when God commanded Adam not to eat of the tree of good and evil. Therefore it was Adams responsability to tell Eve. So Adam disobeyed God and Eve disobeyed her husband. Adam and Eve both decided to disobey God thus Rebellion and deciept were the weapons of Satan.

[1 Corinthians 11:3] "But I want you to know that the head of every man is Christ, the head of the woman is the man, the head of Christ is God."

The second Adam Jesus, will not disobey God and the second Eve, the bride of Christ will not disobey her husband Jesus. Neither will His bride be decieved. All will stay in unity.

1 Corinthians 15:45.

Romans 4:8,10. "But God demonstrates His love towards us, in that while we were still sinners, Christ died for us. Much more than having now been justified by the blood we shall be saved from wrath through Him. For if we were enemies we were reconciled to God through the death of His Son, much more having been reconciled, we will be saved by His life."

Jesus wants to share His life with us. It is again based on strength and weakness. We give Him our weaknesses of sin and hopelessness and spiritual death. We turn from our works of darkness and look to Him who has no weaknesses and begin to be delivered and strengthened and given eternal life by Him and His spirit He gave us when we received Him. In return we give Him our love and loyalty and thanksgiving for what He has done for us. Our enemies are now His enemies. He takes our weakness; we take His strength. He will give us whatever we need to make our lives full.

Jesus said in John 10:10. "The thief does not come except, to steal, and to kill, and to destroy. But I have come that they may have life, and that they may have it and more abundantly.

What will Jesus do for us?

Galatians 5:22, 24

But the fruit of the spirit is love, joy, peace, longsuffering, kindness, goodness faithfulness, gentleness, self-control. Against such there is no law."

He will work these characteristics into us. It is His nature. It is heaven's atmosphere.

He will only do this for those who are betrothed to Him in a covenant. Born again.

He gets us prepared for heaven here, to get to the marriage supper of the Lamb (Revelation 19: 6, 9).

The Holy Spirit is a deposit in our spirit that we have a covenant with God and Jesus. A guarantee of our new heavenly home.

2nd Corinthians 1:22.

"who has also sealed us and given us the spirit in our hearts as a guarantee. He has not left us alone."

2nd Timothy 1:7. "For God has not given us a spirit of fear, but of power, and love and a sound mind."

1st John 4:18. "There is no fear in love, but perfect love cast out fear, because fear is torment, but he who fears has not been made perfect in love."

If you don't want to fear anything anymore, be filled with God. There is no fear in God who is perfect love. God in you cannot be defeated. You are given authority as a child of God. Your size, strength, age, gender, intelect, looks, color of skin or nationality dont matter. God gives you authority based on relationship. You are now in Gods family. Princes and Princesses of the king all have some degree of authority in this world.

If then you are a child of the King, God, will He not supply your needs as His child? You now have the authority He gave you to ask for what you need and want according to His word, The bible. Here is the scripture for that.

[Phillipians 4:19] "And my God shall supply all your need according to His riches in glory by Christ Jesus."

Satan succeeded in breaking the relationship we had with God in the garden, the beginning of mankind. We became vulnerable, fearful. We then went into survival mode. Everything man did after that had to be fought and worked for by his own strength. So the weak were vulnerable to the strong. Whoever could produce fear into the population could control the population. Dictators always had armies to force their will through fear of death on the population so they could be ruler and live extravagant lives. Dictators today get in high positions in government and then make unjust laws to control the people through fear of breaking the law. God loves just laws. Fear and torment are satanic. Narcissism!! Is an evil demon spirit allowing other demons to join in with it to destroy and control people.

God hates all these things, He wants you on His side so He can protect you.

If you want to be victorious in your life, walk with Jesus. Jesus has a taylor made life for you and will personally work with you if you will listen to His instruction, as you will see as you read this example of one life changed by Him in the next chapters.

Enjoy the book.

Chapter 2

My Testimony before Salvation

I am a born-again spirit filled believer now and have followed the Lord for over thirty-four years. I was made whole by the Lord back in July of 1985 when I received him while in the living room of my house after hearing a TV evangelist preach salvation through Jesus Christ. I was twenty-five years old. It sure didn't start that way.

I was born in September 1959 the first born of four kids. I was born in Neenah, Wisconsin, in Theda Clark Hospital. My parents moved down from Upper Michigan for work because jobs were scarce where they were from. Iron mines used to be the main jobs of that region, and they died out.

Like anybody starting out, we lived in apartments for a while until my dad could get the first house. I was told I had a fetish for throwing silverware out the window to watch them hit the ground.

Like any kid I wanted to be loved and feel stable and see home as a place of refuge. But it wasn't exactly like that. When a kid is born the first people to influence that kid is the parents. The kid being born is like a blank page that has to be written on. We get our ideas, influences beliefs, and some of our personality traits from our parents. But most of all, us kids trust our parents. I believed they know everything, and everything they said was right. Spiritually speaking, whatever the parents allow in the house, whether it is good or evil, the kids are also covered and influenced by the same spirits. They are the God-given authority to the child.

Anger some time s rage, seemed to be the standard tool for my dad to address a lot of things, yet he was a good provider, a very confusing mix for a kid. Everything that came from my parents' mouths I thought was right, so when I was called names and hit for seemingly small things, my self-worth was going down fast. I had nothing else to base it on. I already was becoming a confused emotional wreck and wasn't even going to school yet. Being hit is what I hated the most because there was so much rage that I felt death, and my dad was so much bigger I knew there was no way to defend myself. I just hoped it would be short. With someone in rage there is no way to know how far the punishment will go.

On this issue I would like to say that spankings and discipline of kids is vital and biblical. Proverbs 13:24 says, "Who ever spares the rod hates his son, but he who loves him is diligent to discipline him."

There was hate, anger, rage, and love too in the house, and it was getting to me. I had a lot of fear because I didn't know where a place of peace was. So I carried my fears to grade school. I was a recluse and kept to myself. School posed a threat to me just like home. I know now after being saved that there is a spirit of fear. I know that this is what got in me in my young life to torment me. The Lord delivered me of it later.

This was an odd mix because my dad could be real nice too. We would go to parks and swimming, and he was real dedicated family man. He would buy us candy just like any parent. When my dad was kind, he was great. He was generous. It really confused me

As time went on verbal abuse and humiliation took its toll on me to not trust! My brother was born sixteen months after me. I loved him, though we fought like brothers do. We had a lot of fun. He was going through abuse some times too that I could watch happen that made my blood boil because I loved my brother. I was older so I remembered these things.

Proverbs 18:21 says "Life and death are in the power of the tongue."

We are made in the image of God. Our words produce things when they are spoken because they are spirit released through the mouth. So you can curse people or bless them. Words can destroy or build because they get inside of the person you are speaking them to. We have all been hurt by words or built up by them. Most of our interaction with people are through words. People become friends through words being spoken to each other heart to heart because they are spirit. This is why we harden our hearts towards people who would injure us with their words so they don't get to the heart and do some real damage. My dad chose a lot words that destroyed and didn't build up.

This created a low view of myself, like something was wrong with me, not even going to school yet. Yet I was still always wanting his approval. Just one smile of approval would have been enough. Then one day my brother and I were just wandering around the house like kids do, we were in my parents' bedroom while my parents were doing dishes; my mom was washing and my dad was drying. I was about to give my dad a sample of what was coming the next sixteen years. I was getting a hard heart already at this young age. This was a beginning of wanting revenge.

Suddenly I saw my mom's pin cushion sitting on the dresser with all kinds of weapons in it—pins. My mind started working: there was my little brother, pins, and my dad's back to us. This was looking pretty good! Now I was the brains of the outfit because I was older, and when there was a dangerous mission, what better thing to do but send your little brother out on point to be sure that the idea I had was a good one. If he gets killed, it was bad idea, and it was a good thing I didn't do it. Am I right?

I said, "Hey, Ray, do you want to do something funny?" He said "Yeah." He had a smile from ear to ear on his face; he was all in the plan and didn't even hear my perfect plan yet. I took a pin and handed it to him and said, "Go and stick this pin into dad's butt!" He said "should I?" I said yeah, it will be funny! So my obedient partner in crime ran over there without hesitation. I was impressed while I stood back and watched my scheme unfold; he reached up, because he was short and hit the target perfectly! Infraction completed!! Target acquired!

That's when things got exciting and lively! My dad started hollering and yelling at the same time; it was a mixture. My brother bolted into the living room, and his shadow said wait for me! I saw his skeleton leave his body—he was moving!! He had left the pin in the butt. Meanwhile my dad threw the dish rag in the air and started dancing around the kitchen, I saw the polka, the moon walk, and some dance moves that I have never seen before or since. He was really wanting to get that pin out, and finally he got it out! My mom said what happened? Anxiously, my dad said, "That little @#%$&% stuck a pin in my #@$%$@.

My mom doubled over laughing. Meanwhile I was thinking how terrible it is for me to die at such a young age. I was sure my plan was going to be uncovered, but strangely enough it wasn't. I walked out of the room looking innocent and acting, like what kind of a son would do such a thing to you dad?! But it all blew over, and my brother didn't even get in trouble. I was four or five, and my brother was three or four years old.

I went to safety school for three days before kindergarten. I was left there and I had tormenting fear. I didn't trust anybody, especially strangers. I couldn't learn a thing I was to tormented. I did notice how I was different from the other kids though because they were interacting with each other, and I couldn't bring myself to do that. All I knew was my brother. I didn't trust anybody! The torment from home was now on me, and it was affecting my life in public. Demonic oppression.

I started going to kindergarten and noticed the same problem. I didn't want to interact with kids, but with some I did, the quiet ones who seemed to need a friend too. This trend continued on through grade school. I know now that beatings were the thing I was trying to avoid.

The way things were at home was the same, good providing but continual verbal cut downs and hitting below the neck, areas where it couldn't be seen. I had no confidence in public; I really thought I was below the average human, so when someone talked to me, it was a real treat, especially when someone was nice, because as you know school kids are generally not very kind to each other. I was slowly building up bitterness, anger, and hate, the attributes I was exposed to at home. I was getting meaner as well; sin was getting a grip on me, and it was producing a sarcastic mouth, criticism, unforgiveness, hate, and antisocialism. I was still in grade school while all this was happening. Going to church didn't help because what I was hearing talked about in church wasn't changing my life at all. I didn't take it seriously. Learning sin started at home, but now I was hooked and doing my own sin by my own decisions. I had my own evil heart. All of us are born with a sinful heart.

These are the devil's lying tactics: verbal and physical abuse being inflicted by someone who is supposed to love me to the point that I despised myself and how low I was. And then I started to become like what I hated, and then Satan would also whisper and condemn me about how low I was to people and mean, and then as a result no one wanted to be a friend. There was no real good thought coming to me to change my course. So it was a two-edged sword for Satan to destroy me and keep me from God in my future. I had unforgiveness and bitterness. My parents were good providers; we got bikes and swimming lessons, and I had a stay-at-home mom. Great mom.

We must remember that kids are just small people who feel what adults feel. They have a soul, a spirit, and a conscience just like adults but don't know how to handle what they are feeling. Many times the rebellion of kids is a reaction to the injustice or pain they feel and don't know how to deal with it. They have no outlet to relieve it. Their hearts can get hard toward the parent. But equally kids have their own self will and can't just do what they want either; we are called to raise up a child in the way he should go and when he is old, he will not depart from it. Love is what we need. Love corrects and gives consequences to rebellion, but also builds up.

My parents liked to go places and see things, so we were always in the car going somewhere. The highlight of my life happened one day. We went to Wisconsin Dells, and my dad was nice enough to put me and my brother on a Bell 47 helicopter ride. The old mash style helicopters. My dad was supposed to come, but the pilot said he was too heavy, so a skinny guy got in.

I was in heaven. I fell in love with helicopters right there before we even landed. It was fantastic. That's all I thought about. From that time on. All I wanted was to be a helicopter pilot. I would get the same books on helicopters out of the grade school library over and over again every week. I never had anything I truly loved that motivated me before.

Naturally, when the boys who want to be number 1 in the eyes of the class, they go after other kids to prove how tough they are. I wound up in some fights because I had to fight; they didn't give me any choice. I was rolling around in a fight in a classroom and rolling around on the street in front of the Catholic church. The one thing I noticed is that I could fight and walk away from it though, something I never had confidence for before.

During grade school this being a Catholic school there was a need for altar boys during mass, so some of us joined and learned to do masses and help the priests. I liked it a little, but it didn't do anything as far as my salvation. I did some morning masses as well as Sundays. But as time went on I started drinking some of the wine that the priests had me put away and would stagger home. I liked that! I had no fear of God at all but knew He was there, but He seemed to be unreachable and probably didn't even know my name. He wasn't a God I could talk to. I want to add that even with all the trouble I was causing and rebellion to my parents and police, I did still try to do right at home; we did chores and shoveled the sidewalks and drive ways.

Mr. Bokowski was an old retired gentleman who was our next-door neighbor. As I was growing up, we would sit outside on the steps and he sat on his steel lawn chair, and we would talk for a long time. He was a great guy. He would come outside I think and wait for us kids to come out. We would do his snow shoveling of his drive way as he got older, and he would take my brother and me down into his basement after shoveling where there were no witnesses. He had a refrigerator there full of beer and would hand us fourteen year olds a cold one, though he would never give us two. He said all the time, "If you work like men, you should drink like men!" I knew men drank more than one beer, but he didn't want to send us home pickled, singing polkas and country music. He said my parents would kill him.

My brother Ray was my best friend, and I was happy with that. It was not very easy for me to make friends, and when I made one, they usually didn't stick around long. I was too mean. So I got used to being alone a lot, and the activities that we did we kept from our parents so they wouldn't have a heart attack about some of the things we were doing. If you don't focus on anything good, no good can come out of you.

This was my case. I was getting full of the sins of the flesh. By now I had a hard heart and a lot of disrespect for people. My brother and I were a two-man band, and although my dad and I were not close, he let us try different things, one of which was to take his Jon boat with a 7-hp motor into the city channel and motor around in it except that the channel had boating laws: you can't just go where you want. I was about twelve, and my brother about eleven years old. We were in the channel chasing ducks around trying to get them by the neck in front of a restaurant full of people on the channel. Well here comes the cops; they called us in and sent us home to our dad. Now my dad knew the police because he was a fireman, and they work together, so whenever we pulled something with the cops, it was an embarrassment to my dad. My dad sent us to boater safety training after that.

I was now in junior high and was starting to suffer from depression also even though we were doing our undercover fun things. My brother and I got interested in stick matches one day along with a friend of my brother's and we started lighting small fires by the railroad tracks and putting them out. Then I had an idea; let's go and light dried Christmas trees on fire by the city garage. What a good idea! And as we were gone and started some trees on fire, we went back to my brother's friend's house, and his mom said, "Go home; the cops are looking for you." She said we started a grass fire, and the fire department had to come and put it out. "You're kidding!" I said anxiously. She said no! So we were taken to the police station and handed over to my dad who was a fireman; they figured that was a better choice than booking us.

My dad being a lieutenant in the fire department was invited annually to the captain's cottage up north and along with their families. We were not used to being in the country and having more freedom. I was really bad, possessed and with no regard for people in general. I was given a bb gun to go shooting with at the cottage. Being full of the devil and just plain evil, I saw my dad walking through the screen door of the cottage, and I thought what if I shot at him; it wouldn't reach him anyway at this distance. Boy, was I wrong! I drew on him and fired; there was no reaction, and I thought, see it didn't reach him. Later he caught me alone and showed me the mark on his arm; that bb hit right where I aimed; I really underestimated the velocity of the bb. I shot a hole through the screen and into his arm. There was no love lost between my dad and me at that time in my life. He gave me a hard swift kick and had some choice words for me.

But that wasn't the end of my continuous infractions with the bb gun. They also had an outhouse on the property—no bathroom in the house. A lady went in there, so I thought it would be funny to shoot the outhouse while she was in there. She started screaming, so I cleared out. The following year we were invited back, and I started shooting the outhouse again when a guy was in there. He started cussing. Our family was never invited back up there again.

I had no respect for people or property and didn't have a reason to, but I had no joy and a lot of depression. I turned to music as my friend; ever since I was a kid we always listened to the AM radio, which was like a friend to me. I started listening to the band Kiss. They were the new thing coming out at that time and were so different than other bands. I liked their rebellion to the culture and started to follow them. I idolized them and joined the Kiss army. I went to three or four of their concerts and got a guitar pick from Gene Simmons thrown to me. I made them a leader in my life that gave me confidence to rebel against the people around me. I thought it would give me confidence and self-worth but it didn't. I couldn't shake the dark cloud I was under. I even met a guy named Mike Elliot, a Gibson guitar rep who met Kiss many times to sell Gibson's latest guitars to. He reassured me that they were just guys like you and me. But I still idolized them. I realized that I was looking for something worth living for, something bigger than myself.

We lived in the city, and my brother and I got minibikes that we bought. But in the city there was no place to ride, so we would find trails far away by subdivisions being built and ride there, and many times we were caught by the cops for riding on the public streets. We were getting on a first-name basis with them. We would take a bb gun and go to the oval race track and shoot each other below the waist as we drove by with our minibikes. One time we were on a country highway on a Honda, and the cops came up behind us and put his lights on and got on the speaker and said "pull over."

We took off into the woods next to the highway as fast as we could, and the cop pursued us up to the woods. We laid down the bike and lay in the woods and watched him. He was on the loud-speaker warning us to come out now. Then he left. Then we waited for a while until we thought it was safe. When we were ready to go, we looked behind us and there was that cop driving his car in the field from the other way to ambush us. So we did what any desperate person who didn't want to get caught would do—we ran! We got back on the motorcycles, got back on the highway the way we came, and went and hid behind a building until the coast was clear; he kept looking for us for a while.

Even with all the fun things we were doing, I was still suffering from depression; nothing seemed to be the answer to it—not music or breaking the law. The more sin I did, the more depressed I got; evil was stealing my life and joy. We didn't tell our parents anything! I was about fourteen years old and in junior high. By now my attitude at home was bad to where my dad couldn't stand me. I was in rebellion and rotten, and he did not like what he saw. I was just like him. The sins of the fathers are passed down from generation to generation, but my sin was my own by my own decisions until it was broken by the intervention of Jesus Christ coming saving me and being born again and saved. This is how you break generational curses. Just because something is in your family doesn't mean you have to have it. Under Christ, it's a whole new set of rules. Curses are broken if you will believe the promises.

Some of the best times we had with our dad was deer hunting every year wth him. Lots of laughs.

My brother and I were mentally so screwed up that we were sent to a psychologist for a few sessions. He surmised that the problem was communication with my dad. Dad sat in the sessions so I couldn't be free to talk. And he recommended that I go to sessions to the mental health facility. I went to one session and could quickly see it wasn't going to do anything. They couldn't get rid of the problems I had. I was angry inside; there was no justice coming. Guilty people who afflicted me seemed to get away with it, and the bitterness and anger and unforgiveness and guilt from my own doings to others made me hate myself. What was the answer to all this? I was a ticking time bomb. Later as you read you will find out that there is an answer. A relief.

My brother and I were really into all-star wrestling TV shows. We even wrestled with our dad until he started losing; we were getting bigger and stronger. I still didn't have much confidence, but we liked to wrestle, so we would put on contests at the gym balcony with other guys during lunch break at the junior high school, and Ray and I would usually take care of business, I was strong. The wrestling coach asked me if I wanted to be on the team, but I said no. I was more interested in our after-school activities.

All this was happening in junior high, and it was there I found my first love, Kacie W. She was a sweetheart and was good to me. I want to give her honor in this book. My brother was a Casanova, and people knew he was my brother, so one day at the gym some girls came up to me, and one wanted to give a note to my brother and handed it to me to give to him. I said yes and took it. One of her friends started liking me; this was Kacie, and later we started talking and hit it off. I fell in love with her quickly. But my lack of confidence came out double time when it came to girls. I was afraid if she knew the real me, she would hit the road. She really liked me, so the problem was me. I would tell her a story that she would see through and say, "Don't lie" but I couldn't over time give her what she wanted. She approached me honestly one day and said she had someone else. I said okay and acted like it didn't matter. It tore me to pieces because I knew it was me, and I didn't know what to do about it. It took a long time to get over it.

This did not help my self-esteem at all or confidence. I could not find what I was good for. The only thing that kept me going was what we did after school. We speared fish at the channel, under the paper mills, and fished for perch at the dam. I had a paper route because I was too young to work anywhere else yet. After the breakup I got into more music and rebellion. I had to have something to fill my empty life.

When I was seventeen, I was so bad and knew I was screwed up, even entertaining the lie of suicide. I went to the Catholic church by myself alone when nobody but me and God were there. And I said, God, my life is a mess. I need your help, whatever you can do. I stayed there awhile and then left, but when I left I felt different, lighter. I don't know what happened, but God had his hand on me. I didn't get saved until 1985. This was about 1977. I will say that going to the Catholic building isn't what did it; it was a soul crying out for God's help and seeing my need for Him. I could have done the same thing in my car or standing in the back yard or in a cave. God is everywhere. But that's what I was taught.

At this time in my life I was seventeen years old and had a job at the bowling alley, filling coolers and working on bowling machines during league night, keeping them running. Later I became a mechanic, the main mechanic's assistant. Because of my background at home and seeing what bullying was like, I hated bullies!! I hated how they went after the weaker people, and parents can be bullies too if correction is taken too far. So I couldn't stand to see it.

We had an incident one night when the bowling alley was getting ready to close. Some drunken guy's wife came to the lanes to get her husband. He took her to the foyer of the door way and was slamming her against the wall. I told another guy that worked there, let's go stop him! But he didn't want anything to do with it. Then the guy dragged his wife outside and had her on the gravel parking lot sitting on top of her; my blood boiled and I couldn't stand it anymore.

I went out there and told him I was gonna kick his @#$%@. Well, it was on! He came at me and hit me in the jaw and I returned the favor; we were having a fist fight, and his wife was trying to break it up. We kept up but he was too strong for me and was eventually on me on the ground. I was seventeen; he looked to be about forty-five. But the bottom line was that it stopped him from doing any more damage. His wife had to be taken to the emergency room for stiches. I just hated bullies. By this time I was what you would call a manic depressive.

One night my parents came to the bowling alley to visit, and after work I sat with them and started drinking. My dad and I started having words, and I was yelling at him in front of the whole bowling alley. All this pent-up anger even surprised me with how mad I was. A lot of anger was pent up in me. I wacked the beer glass across the room, and it broke in my hand and cut my hand. I went stomping out of there and got in my Ford Maverick in the middle of winter without my windshield scraped clean from ice, just a little spot to see through. Then the cops pulled me over for the windshield. He saw I was drinking and was going to arrest me, but he saw my hand bleeding and asked my name. He said it looks like you had enough trouble for one night. Leave the car here and walk home. I was thankful.

Satan had his weapons out against me, knowing I was getting closer to salvation. There was this guy who I met through a friend who was a lay person in the Catholic church. He was older but was friendly, so we all got together once in a while, and he would talk to me about my problems and other stuff in general, and I was looking for any answers I could find. This went on for over a year until one day he put the moves on me, and he turned out to be homosexual. How patient they are until they earn your trust. I cleared out of there in a hurry. There was no place of peace, and my trust for people wasn't getting any better.

When I got out of junior high and into high school, my brother and I bought a 40-hp wood boat and motor from a local drug dealer. He needed the money, $300.00, and we wanted the boat.

We were taking up skiing; we lived by the channel that went out to Lake Winnebago.

On my paper route I had an old customer who lived on the channel and had a big yard. I approached her and asked if we could build a dock to tie our boat to. She said yes. Her name was Mrs. Coerper. She was a school teacher at Hortonville High School. We would sit and have talks, and she was a great listening ear during those turbulent times in my life. We had a blast with that boat and skied all over that lake. We took people out who never got a chance to try it. We would dress up and ski past the swimming area. I would put on a football outfit and our friend Rusty. Nick, named #*$, would put on an old dress from his mom's junk.

Mrs. Coerper's son, was Rodney, to whom I want to give honor. He was one of the first born-again persons I ever met. He visited from time to time because he went to college. He was a gentle soul. We made fun of him under our breath. I was bad, but I still liked him.

Mrs. Coerper let us stay at her house to visit even if she wasn't there because she liked the company, and we would do little chores for her she couldn't do because she was a widow. One day I was making out with a girl I liked at her house, and Rodney came up to me and said, "My mom would not approve if she were here," and he was right. I threatened him because I felt convicted about it, and he said if you want to hit me go ahead. I told him he wasn't worth it, which was the wrong thing for me to say. I didn't touch him, but God takes up the case of his believers, and I wasn't one of them yet, but Rodney was. We left the house.

Shortly after that there was a half day at school and that girl I had been kissing was breaking up with me. I hated the rejection too much of it in my life, but some of it I brought on myself because of my bad attitude. I was too young to buy alcohol.

So I planned that after school I was going to go into my dad's, homemade dandelion wine in the basement, which hadn't been tested yet, and this was the first time my dad had ever made this swill; he didn't know if it was any good. I planned on getting drunk! Then I'd go to my ex-girlfriend's house and tell her how I really felt. So I went home, went downstairs, went into the pantry, opened a bottle of that sewer water wine—it's dandelion wine, but it tasted like what sewer water would taste like if you had it, I don't know! Never tried sewer water. I got drunk fast. Now I am a certifiable jerk to begin with, think how bad I was then. So I got on my bike— thank God I couldn't drive yet—and I zig-zagged all the way to her house. The wine hasn't taken its full affect yet, but I was getting drunker as I got to her house.

I got on the porch and started pounding on the door come out here, you @#$%. Her dad came out instead and tried to calm me down, and I started throwing things off the porch acting like a demon. But I was getting drunker still. Then some people from across the street came over, and they knew me. They owned the archery lanes we shot league at. So they took me over to their house and put me in a bed. I puked on their bed, and they called my dad at work. He was on a twenty-four-hour shift at the fire dept. He came and hauled me home and threw me in the bed, but they were concerned if I poisoned myself. They called the ambulance and hauled me off to the emergency room. The doctor said I think he will be all right, but he's gonna have one h- of a hangover tomorrow. I started talking about my failures to the doctor and all the things that were bothering me because I was loaded, and all restraint was gone. I was telling them what was eating me up inside, but no one understood. All the doctor said was that "woman were like buses; there's one every half hour."

Then the next day -ooooohhhhhh! I had a hangover that would make an NFL player lay on the floor, cry like a baby, and suck his thumb. I was sick!!! I was puking my toes up.

It felt like a .38 caliber bullet in my head, not that I ever experienced that before. The harder I puked, the harder my dad laughed.

I lived. But I remembered later in life how I treated Rodney concerning that girl. Satan had his way with me. Do not persecute Christians; there is a payday for you even if it's not right away, unless you repent; then you are forgiven.

But even with all this I was empty inside. I would go home at night and still feel empty and lonely; nothing would satisfy. My dad got the boat fever and bought a 40-hp fiberglass ski boat. He was nice enough to let us use it once in a while. We were still teenagers, and my parents planned a camping trip to Pine Air Resort in Eagle River, Wisconsin. We heard that there was a ski show up there called the Chain Skimmers and we put two and two together and decided there was a ski jump too, so we were going to have to try this jump out.

We took the trip up there and got a site next to the water where we could park the boat permanently. We eventually went to the ski show and watched. We figured out that our site was not far from the jump, and they had a nice big competition jump. So after the show the ski team drivers offered free rides in the ski boats. These were professional ski Nautique inboards. We had to be strapped in or we could be thrown out of the boat. It was a blast. Went back to the site for the night.

The next day we got in the boat—Rusty, Ray, and I took off and didn't say where we were going. We headed for the jump. It was on the Chain of Lakes, so it took us a while to get there. We took the rudders off the skies, and Ray practiced without the rudders to see if he could ski without them. He decided to go first, which I didn't mind because if he got killed, then I would know it was a bad idea and that I probably shouldn't take the jump. Am I right?? So we had the ski jump in sight finally!

So we idiots headed toward the jump full power. Ray was already on the skies, I was driving, and Rusty was spotting. We came up next to the jump full speed, then suddenly I noticed emergency marker lights set up on the top of the jump to stop idiots like us from taking the jump when the show isn't using it. Too late! Ray went up the jump and saw the lights at the last minute; he let the rope go and crashed through the lights and went tumbling into the water. So we checked if he was all right, he said yeah, and then I had the idea that we need to get him and get out of there before we get caught. So I drove the boat next to the jump, and we got Ray out of the water, then I noticed that a rope was floating from the jump that anchors the jump. I had cut an anchor rope to the jump with the boat motor propeller. Ooooohhhhhh no!! I said let's get out of here! I backed out and cut another rope, and now the jump was moving and turning. This jump is set up in a certain position for the show. We were dead! The boats that the ski show uses are inboards with the propeller coming out of the keel or bottom. This was a professional competition ski jump, not someone's makeshift back yard variety.

Their boats can't cut the ropes but I was using an outboard, knife blades next to the surface just waiting to cut ropes.

Then it gets better. We heard screaming and hollering from the shore. It was the whole ski team; they saw the whole thing. We never even saw them because we were focused on what we were doing. They said "get over here; we have your boat numbers," so we went over there and were met with less-than-hospitable remarks. They had to take turns. Seems we ruined the show for that night, and it was going to cost us a bundle. They told us it would take scuba gear to re-anchor the ropes to the jump and weren't sure if they could get it done by the show time.

If not we would have to pay for the show. We were having a bad day. So we gave them our campsite address and putted off real slow back to the campsite, knowing that this recent development would have to be communicated to the parents.

We got to the site, and I was in survival mode. I knew Ray or Rusty, weren't going to say anything; they took off, leaving me to take the beating. So I went to ma, they were getting ready to go to town, and I told her what happened and to communicate that to dad on the way to town so he has time to cool off.

Naturally she quietly exploded but agreed. When they came back, of course, there was colorful language. We were never going to touch that boat again and we ruined everything for them. Sometimes that's true. So we waited for the news from the ski show people. Later in the afternoon, two guys showed up from the show and said they fixed the jump in time. They were really nice. They showed us some moves on our discs we had, and talked with us, and handed us a bill for fifteen dollars for rope only. Thank you, thank you, thank you, thank you, thank you, cooled my dad down, and we were in the boat the next day.

I mentioned that we were Catholics, but we as a family did pray every night in our living room to a picture of Jesus, and they were always the repeated prayers of the Catholics—no life to them, just repetition. I was called by God but still didn't know it at that time, but suddenly new prayers would come into my mind and that was different for me because they were not on the beaten path. They were like talking to God prayers. So God kept me alive and out of big trouble until the day I received Him.

I was a senior in high school and full of rebellion and didn't care what people thought. I had it with the world and its control over me. Now I was controlling, fighting control with control. My tennis teacher from gym class called my parents and said I was acting out of control.

I went out for high school football sophomore and junior years, That did not go so well. I needed to start at the junior high level first. So by this time I had no real reason that I could do much of anything in life.

I worked at the bowling alley for the second time as stock person and then worked on the machines all night to keep them running during bowling league nights. This helped my confidence to see I could work on machines and understand their process. Later I became the head mechanic's assistant. I was then able to get my first car, a Ford Maverick.

Out on Lake Winnebago at a certain time during the winter, they will plow a section of ice and on a weekend have four-wheel drive races. I had a friend from high school for a while named Chuck. Chuck and I went out there one night after the races were over and decided to pull each other on a plastic sled behind the car on the open ice. So we took turns, and it was going good, it was my turn to pull Chuck, and I saw a long ice bank. It was an ice shove out in the distance, and I thought it would be a great bank to slam him against, so I headed toward it. As I came alongside there was this blue ice next to it, so as I started on the blue ice, the ice broke under the car; it was thin ice. The car started sinking, then it came back up! The front wheel was braking ice, the back wheels had nothing to ride on, yet the car came back up, and I was able to drive back onto hard ice again. The whole side of the car was caked in ice; it was about 20 degrees out at night. The door was freezing shut. I got out of the car and looked and there was Chuck swimming! I broke so much ice that Chuck was in the water swimming to the other side; it was a big hole. I should have been at the bottom of the lake.

Chuck was stuck on the other side; because he was strong, he was able to pull himself out of the water on the other side. We couldn't find a spot to bring him back to my side. He was starting to get hyperthermia. We kept looking and eventually got him back over to me, and I got him home fast. He was okay! Thank God. Knowing what I know now, I know an angel was sent to lift my car from sinking; there was no physical way for that to happen. I would have been in hell for sure at that time in my life. Jesus was not in my life yet. Later I saw that God had spared my life.

Chuck was my best friend in high school. We hunted, fished, skied, four wheeled, got drunk, got in trouble, shot at each other behind trees, and other stuff. We were deer hunting one day, and nothing was happening. So Chuck decided to climb a tall dead tree and take a look around for deer. I said, that tree won't hold you! He said, "yes it will "no it won't "yes it will "no it won't! So he climbed the tree anyway. I handed him his gun. I was waiting on the ground while he was scoping out the area. Suddenly, snap, crackle—I looked up, and there was Chuck, cartwheeling off the branches on his way down to good old earth. There wasn't a thing I could do about it except eat popcorn and watch the show! I would see what's left when he gets down to the ground. His gun hit the ground first, then him; it was an impressive display of gymnastics. There were no body parts in the tree. So when he finally got to the ground, he was quiet and still in one piece. I said, should we go? He said yeah! We left.

Over the years, I was getting in car accidents. I was well known for falling asleep behind the wheel; it was a spirit of heaviness. I had an incident when I was deer hunting with my dad and brothers. My brother Dan and I were coming back to camp. I fell asleep at highway speeds, and all of a sudden I felt the van pull to the right, and I woke up and found us going down a ditch that was deep enough that the roof of the van was at the level of the road. So I controlled it in the middle of the ditch, but the problem was a four-foot culvert was right in front of us, and I couldn't stop. The only thing I could do was turn hard left and hope for the best. But to my surprise the van climbed back up the hill and back onto the road. The laws of physics were not in play. I shouldn't have been able to do that without the van tipping over. It was a steep climb on a sharp left turn. Later I realized that God had saved me again, even in my ignorance. That culvert could have decapitated us at the level it was or turned the van into a sausage shape. We drove away. My brother's heart rate doubled, and he needed the bathroom after we got back! Obviously he overreacted.

I graduated in 1978 and got a job at a used car lot at first but my distrust for people and my inherent general dislike for people was evident and made it hard to get along with my coworkers. One guy was just joking with me and I told him off in front of everybody.

My heart was really hard. I didn't need anyone. But there was one guy who saw something was wrong with me; he was a mechanic, and he had compassion on me, took time to talk to me, and defused my defenses. He asked me to help him with a break job on a car he was working on. He was really kind to me; he didn't say anything about the Lord, but at that time if there would have been an example of what I would have called a Christian, it would have been him. His name was Steve Stoll. I would like to honor him in this book. I don't take people going the extra mile with me lightly.

I got into martial arts for a while and started working my way up. This was also to give me self-worth and self-confidence. Then I tore my knee in my kicking style. I had to have surgery, and it left my knee not as good as it was. This was before the days of arthroscopic surgery. I never went back because of the risk of reinjuring it.

I started working at the Neenah foundry then around 1980. This was a rough place. We would all go get drunk on our lunch break on Thursdays, including the supervisors. I was so hard and thought people had it out for me that one day a group of guys were standing together and one of them threw his ice at me from his pop cup. So I went over there in front of them all and kicked him right in the butt as hard as I could with my steel toe. I remember feeling bad about it after I did it. I was quick tempered. And later I went and told him I was sorry and I didn't know why I did these things. This is the place I was working when I got saved later, and these guys I was working with got to see the change in me later.

I was also a DJ in a biker bar. I was really into music; it was always part of my life. I knew bands, dates of music, and the songs, so I went to this biker bar that had a DJ system and played music for two years at that place. I got along good with them, partied with them, and bought a new 1975 Norton 850 from the owner. We went on a poker run with them too, and I was working the foundry on days and DJ job on the weekends. The foundry was quite a place, with some of the roughest people I have ever met; a lot of them used to be in prison. I fit right in. I saw some things happen there that people would have been arrested for on the streets.

I got my girlfriend, whom I had been dating for about a year, pregnant and decided to marry her and try to make it go. We were married at the courthouse and had the reception at her parents' garage, along with two half barrels of beer. Never in my thoughts did I think I was going to have a lame wedding like that. Nothing had changed though; my life was still empty, I was grasping at the straws of life looking for the next new thing to bring me satisfaction. The marriage wasn't going well either. She was strong willed, and I was strong willed and didn't trust people. We got along at first. Then we had that Carter recession, and we started having financial problems, and she liked money. I was laid off and was getting unemployment checks that just barely kept us going. We started fighting, and amidst that family infighting our son was born.

Basically my family versus hers was all a recipe for disaster. She would also get the mail and hide unemployment checks on me, but it did no good because I had to sign them. Then one day we had a fight; she refused to let me take our son to visit his grandparents, my parents. So I told her a week ahead that I was going there on Saturday with our son. Saturday came, and I started getting the bag ready to bring the supplies, and while I was doing that, she grabbed our son and locked herself in the bathroom with him. I lost it! I kicked the door in and put my hands around her neck and said "this is what I would like to do to you" but didn't squeeze. Then I took the baby and went. I have never hit a woman. I didn't hurt her.

My brothers and I one day decided we were going to go find deer hunting spots. Now I had a really nice half-ton Ford Econoline van, newly painted, with a good stereo system. There were four of us, my two brothers and one of their friends. We were going to the Menomonee Indian Reservation direction, knowing it's illegal to hunt on Indian land. But we were making a day of it. We brought orange juice and vodka. We knew it was a road trip, not looking for hunting spots. We headed north and started drinking as we went. I was in my van with one guy and my brothers were following in my brother's car. We were all drinking. We went about 60 miles out, having a real good time, stopping here and there, looking at the woods but never really serious about hunting. A good portion of the day had gone by, and we were drunk but could still drive. We stopped at a tavern and decided to have a drink, shoot pool, and start heading back.

Just as we were starting to head back, sleet started falling, the kind that freezes on contact. The roads were iced, the trees were iced. It was not safe to go out at all, much less being drunk. But we had a long drive ahead of us, and I ignored the ice and thought I would just go slow. Bad decision! We started leaving; I was in the lead, my brother behind. The road going out is one of those very hilly roads, up, down, and curves before it straightens out later. So as I was on this road, I noticed I was going about 50 miles an hour, way too fast! I tried to slow down but it was too late. As we were going over the next hill, there was a turn at the bottom, and I knew right away we were going too fast.

So I tried to make the turn, and the van slid sideways down the highway. I was looking at the road through my door glass on my left. Then suddenly the van tipped over on its side and went sliding down the middle of the highway until it came to a complete stop. No one was coming on the highway, no glass was broken accept for a mirror, and we were just fine. Not even a scratch. I was looking up at my passenger, and we were both sober then.

Then I said quick get all the booze bottles out and throw them in the woods and any evidence at all before the cops come. So we crawled out of the van and got rid of the evidence. Then cars started coming and stopping. What are these people doing out here under such bad conditions? They asked "are you okay?" yeah!!

So then more guys came, and my brother came up behind us and pulled over. One guy said, you know with all of us here, we could flip this van back on its wheels! I said yeah let's do it!!

So we tied a rope to my brothers car, and then all of us guys got hold of the roof and lifted the van back on its wheels. I got in, and the van started. One guy said get out of here before the cops come! I said yeah! And thank you everybody. Now I was sober. So we kept going very slow, and as we were going, here came four squad cars with their lights flashing. Someone in those cars must have had a CB radio—because this was before cell phones—or maybe an old mobile phone.

The police pulled me over, gave me a field sobriety test, and arrested me. I was arrested, taken in and processed, then put in jail. I was put in jail within an hour and a half of a major car accident. My brothers left and went somewhere to sober up and get away from the commotion. I remember thinking, they really think I'm dangerous enough to be locked up. I couldn't believe it. I didn't know what was going to happen next. My brothers drank a lot of coffee, came back to the sheriff's office to get me on their own recognizance. They got away with it. God clearly spared my life and my passenger and the lives of the people who showed up later. No injury to anyone. I personally believe that all those people that showed up after the crash were put there by God because of their timing and the fact that by getting the van flipped back minimized the incident.

I went to court and lost my license for three months. So my wife had to drive me to the night club to my DJ job. Just after I lost my license, my wife picked me up after bar closing, and I told her I would drive. She said you don't have your license! But I did anyway. This was the first time after I lost my license. I was driving at the speed limit doing good and suddenly flashing lights came up behind me. I got nervous. It was winter, and the back window was frosted. The cop couldn't see us yet. So I told my wife, I will jump

who has the authority to hold a situation until the police arrive. I had a pickup truck full of beer cans in the back. This did not look good. The guy in the accident went with the deputy to town to get the police. Meanwhile the guy with him stayed with his car, and my girlfriend and I stayed with the truck. So I decided to take the beer cans out and walk down the road and bury them in the woods before the police arrived, right in front of the other passenger of the Volkswagen.

I knew I wasn't drunk but thought I didn't stand a chance of convincing a cop of that with the contraband in the back. Sure enough when the police arrived the driver of the other vehicle gave the cop an earful right away. The first thing the cop does is look in back of my truck for beer cans. He said, where are the beer cans? I said what beer cans? Not the best answer. Then he said to the passenger who saw me get rid of them, where did he take them?

So he led the cop down the road to look for the spot I buried the cans. They couldn't find them. So he looked over the accident, and we gave statements as to what happened. Then he gave me a field sobriety test. I passed without a single problem. He was mad because I lied about the cans. So he arrested me and put me in the squad car. My girlfriend followed in my truck to town where they did a breathalyzer test on me that was clean. So they let me go.

The accident report must have turned out to be his fault because I was never contacted about it again.

Nobody at the campsite knew where we were all this time, and it was late when we finally got back to the site. My girlfriend's friend who came with us said that she thought I killed her somewhere in the woods. "Thanks a lot I said." But I look back now and realize that I didn't see myself the way others saw me, because that comment surprised me that she would think that.

My girlfriend and I would go up to the Moe Lake Indian Reservation for a once a year party bash in my old beat-up truck. There were very few rules there because the reservation was not under some of the Wisconsin laws. So we listened to bluegrass music and drank hard liquor. They brought in some big-name bands, and then when it was over, we would barely remember coming home. People were passed out on the ground, and we all would just walk around their bodies. It was a little like the wild west. We could smoke weed in the open.

In this night club of 1,500, I was emcee. Of filthy contests of all kinds, a lot of perverse people came out of the woodwork. Life was still so empty even after all this, the *Post Crescent* newspaper even came out and did a story on our entertainment out there, and had a front page picture of me on the entertainment section with the interview from my brother, so they got both of us in. My brother and I were alike in a lot of ways because he came out of the same lifestyle I did. I loved my brother; we spent a lot of time in the night clubs, which was our second home. We were both DJs and both alcoholics. If we weren't working that night we would be in the bars.

One night at the nightclub my brother got into a serious standoff with his brother-in-law in the bathroom. Both liked to fight, and I've seen them fight. I knew they were not bluffing.

They were getting ready to go at it in the bathroom. My brother pulled the knife and that was the first time I saw it. I had seen him fight before, but he never pulled a knife on someone and went as far to want to kill them. He pulled the knife and started moving towards him, and all I could think of was "he is going to prison." That was unacceptable. He would have ruined his life in 30 seconds. So without thinking I went at him and grabbed the hand with the knife in it and tried to pry it out of his hands, but he wouldn't let go. So I hit his hand against the wall and got the knife out and I got cut. My blood was on the bathroom floor. He had his fist drawn back to hit me, but he never did. He knew I was right. Neither of us had any peace. Fortunately everybody cleared out of the room and let it go.

I got my girlfriend pregnant, and we both knew we didn't want the baby. She wanted an abortion, and I didn't try to stop her. I payed for the abortion and didn't put up a fight. It was both our faults. I could not believe the direction my life was going. I was doing things that I never thought in my wildest dreams I would ever do. We couldn't stop having sex even after killing that baby. Both our hearts were really hard.

God in his mercy was getting ready to start pulling me in. Things were changing, and I got my girlfriend pregnant again. I didn't know what we were going to do. And then God intervened and shut down the pregnancy. The pregnancy just stopped, and she went back to normal. And we knew she was pregnant; her body was already changing. It was not a miscarriage. But from that time on God was beginning to separate us. The call on my life was getting closer.

I was working for a commercial roofing company at the time because it was the only work available because of the recession. I was laid off from the foundry, so I was a DJ at night and a roofer in the day. I was driving an old Ford pickup truck that had different color doors on it, was rusted, wooden bumper, wooden flatbed—a very ugly truck, I had to put a shift kit in it. It was a piece of junk, but it was all I could afford.

One day as I always parked it on the street in front of my girlfriend's house because there was no spot in the driveway, a drunk guy came out of his house yelling at me to quit parking this truck in front of his house! He didn't want anyone to think that he owned it.

Things were mighty low at this point. Broke, lousy job, divorced, alcoholic, a truck that barely ran: sin had me by the throat. It took everything from me. When we sin, it takes away our will power and self-worth. Walking around in continual condemnation, hardening our hearts so we don't feel the pain and emptiness of it. There was no vision of the future, just day-to-day living. I needed goals, purpose that was constructive.

When the devil has you because you don't have Jesus, if you're not doing anything wrong, then the devil will bring up the past to stir guilty feelings to keep us condemned, or use someone to remind you of your past. This is used in marriages alot. Bringing up the past in order to control the spouse. We are easy to control that way. Demons need us to live inside of us, to carry out their wicked desires. Demons are disembodied spirits who need human vessels to carry out physical destruction on the earth. Demons can and will enter you if they can if you open doors to them. It always starts with the thoughts we let in that can come from demon influence or our own wicked flesh desires. [Galations 5:17,21]

Jesus delivered a multitude of people who were demon possessed and oppressed, some with many demons in one person. The same is true today; there is no difference, just a different time, different generation.

My girlfriend wanted to go out to the bar one night, and I just caught a commercial on TV that was doing a promo add for *Jesus of Nazareth*, the movie that was going to be showing the next three nights on TV because it was long. I told her "you go; I'm staying and watching *Jesus of Nazareth*. The next three nights. I was compelled to watch. I couldn't wait until night time to see the next episodes. As I watched, I could feel my heart softening, and I said I want to know this guy. I was crying from time to time, and my heart was feeling different. I was not saved yet, but it was God moving in me to watch that movie to move me along to eventual salvation.

My girlfriend and I moved to a house in Neenah Wisconsin. Times were getting better, and I got called back to the foundry from the layoff, so the money got better, but Jesus was on my mind more than ever before. She was getting a little bothered by it; after all we were drinking and partying buddies.

Her dad wanted me to marry her, but God kept us from going through with it. I was getting convicted about living with her without being married and having sex without marriage. When I would tell her about it, she would say what's going on with you?

I don't know I said. It never bothered me before, but Jesus was drawing closer although I didn't know it at the time.

I was invited to Canada to fish with my girlfriend's dad and a group on White Fish Lake, and so we took her dad's car and boat, and the three of us went to Canada. Jesus was on my mind strong, and I had a hard time sharing a room with my girlfriend in front of everybody there because we weren't married. My conscience was coming alive.

We caught a ton of perch. We weren't really after game fish— walleye, northern— because you can't take many home with you across the Canadian border, but you can take fifty perch or more per person across the border so you can have some fish fries at home. One day her dad and I went fishing alone, and I told him that I didn't think it was right for his daughter and me to live together any more, he said "I suppose you're right" I just felt compelled to tell him that. He was a good guy and treated me well, but I knew that the parting of ways was coming between her and me, I and wanted to be honest with her dad. We finished our Canadian trip; it was great, a lot of fish, and I saw a moose.

My girlfriend was a good seamstress, so we made outfits for a Halloween costume contest. I went as Ace Frehley of Kiss. She went as a groupie. I had the elevator shoes and everything. We went to night clubs to enter contests with our costumes. I felt stupid though, and it wasn't as much fun as I thought it would be. Bar fun was fading away for me. It was the real last night out into the bars we did; it was coming to an end.

I just wanted to say that this is a portion of my life. I did much more than this, but these are some of the highlights. God had pulled me out of a very wicked life, and he can do that for you too. The unforgivable sin is not receiving Jesus as your Savior and repenting of your sin after He has provided it for you. He wouldn't have done it if we didn't need it, and to reject it is serious and deadly. Be wise: receive Him in your heart. God loves you extremely and wants to be your Savior and not your judge. Because He is Holy and can't live with sin, He must judge sin and condemn it and those who want to practice it. Jesus needs your permission to enter your life. He is a gentlemen.

So we still were living together, and she was going out on her own and would ask me to watch her little girl, and I would. I quit the DJ business in the night clubs. Then one day my girlfriend came up to me and said she couldn't take it anymore and wanted to move out back to her home town, Appleton. She was feeling the separation of flesh and spirit; God was drawing closer to me. So she moved out.

I bought her a car so she had reliable wheels, but after she left I was relieved and not sad. So I continued working and just going home. I was still drinking, I was a full-blown alcoholic. I was going down to the liquor store and getting hard liquor for the weekends, and I drank beer on the weekdays so I could go to work.

Then it happened! I was watching TV in mid-July of 1985. I was sitting in my house by myself, and a TV preacher came on TV talking about Jesus and being saved. It was Jim Bakker before his ministry fell.

He was talking about being saved and being born again. I said "so that's what you have to do." For the first time in my whole search for God I finally understood how to be saved.

He read Romans 10:9–10:

9, "That if you confess with your mouth the Lord Jesus and believe in your heart that God has raised him from the dead, you shall be saved.

10, for with the heart one believes unto righteousness, and with the mouth confession is made unto salvation."

I believed it!! So the preacher said if anyone wants to receive Jesus and salvation wherever you are hearing this, "just pray this salvation prayer with me right now and you will be saved. I knelt in my living room by myself, just the Holy Spirit and me. I was twenty-five years old when this took place.

I said something like this: God I thank you for forgiving my sins and cleansing me with the blood of Jesus, and I ask that Jesus comes into my heart and be the Lord of my life. The power of God hit me in the chest as the Holy Spirit had entered me. I felt clean and something was going on in my chest, I was getting a new heart as it was promised in Ezekiel 36: 25–27:

25, "Then I will sprinkle clean water on you and you shall be clean; I will cleanse you from all your filthiness and from all your idols.

26, I will give you a new heart and put a new spirit within you; I will take the heart of stone out of your flesh and give you a heart of flesh.

27, I will put my spirit within you and cause you to walk in my statutes, and you will keep my judgments and do them."

This is a prophesy of what God would bring to us after Jesus's death and resurrection. I experienced it in my living room; I could feel the physical change and the spiritual change. God gave me a heart of flesh in place of a heart of stone, just like the Bible verse says. All I had to do was believe and receive, and God did the rest. Glory to God forever!

Salvation is for all who will receive it, no matter what you have done. It is for you!!!

In closing, I took accountability for my actions and thoughts before God! I want to say my mind was a garbage heap of evil thoughts that turned to evil deeds. What you focus on is what you will become like. I wrote this book to show the progression of sin in a life and the devastating consequences that the devil and my own evil flesh desires can lead a person to.

I was without hope, without self-esteem or self-worth, without love. My sins were many. I was delivered of perversity, hate, murder, hopelessness, manic depression, alcoholism, unforgiveness, bitterness, violent temper, fear that manifested in control, and guilt, just to name some. Nothing is too big for God to handle or forgive. He is still working on me. The more you walk with Jesus, the more these things will fall away and be replaced by the character of Jesus as you listen to Him and continue with Him. It is his very life in us and His power that makes us free. Then you are free. He is getting us ready for heaven and eternity. There is no sin done on the earth that cannot be forgiven.

Sin is the enslavement that we are born into and practice all our lives unless we receive Jesus; then He will break the chains of our habits, perversities, lies, and more. When we are born into sin, we don't know anything else until the gospel is preached and you see that God had made a way of escape. This is light, showing the way of escape. The Bible is light! Spoken truth by God! When we hear it, it should give us an indication of what and who we are and what we need. Because the light has come. The bible trouble shoots our condition and then gives us the remedy.

You are not loving somebody by accepting their sin and perversity, calling it their own way or their own life. Leaving someone in this state is automatically sending them to hell, not because of the sin, but because of not receiving Jesus to get rid of the sin and put them in right standing with God. Once they have heard, then the decision is theirs. They choose their own path. If you are saved, do not be afraid to be a light. Truth and light manifest what's in a room, both good and bad. We stand for what's right because we stand with Jesus, the ultimate Savior and judge. A lot of people avoid the word of God because if they hear it, it is truth! They will see themselves in a way they may not like because of the need for repentance.

Anything goes in darkness, and anything can be done in darkness, but when light comes, it requires change because people see what you're doing. But God's changes will save you. Then you will be the same in private and in public. You will have nothing to hide. Your free.

Nothing of this earth that you can focus on will save you and get you ready for heaven. Focus on Jesus and his Holy Spirit sent to you and me into the earth, get saved, and let Him straighten out your life. He does the work; you do the believing. He is the only one who can get you prepared to meet the Father in heaven. "You can do all things through Christ who strengthens you" (Phil. 4:13), "casting all your cares upon Him for he cares for you" (1 Pet. 5:7).

He has a life and plans for you. Don't wander aimlessly in life. He gives you value, and worth. The world tries to take it from us. The world can't defeat Jesus.

Maybe you are one of those who esteems yourself by your successes in life, your talents, your good looks, loving the admiration of man, thinking, why do I need Jesus? Just know and understand that your life is spiritually still dead. You are still disconnected from God. Man's esteem is a failed substitute for God's favor. Be wise and make a good decision to accept God's free gift of salvation. Be His child. See your need. Success is good in a good thing, but do not let it be your god that you put your whole identity into, forsaking salvation. Anything that you make your god that is not the real and true living God will destroy you to condemnation in hell because there is no eternal life in the false thing you put above Jesus. Nothing on earth has eternal life in it. Only Jesus, who is not of this world as Jesus said in John 17:16:

Here is a scripture for that.

Matthew 19:16, 26:

Now behold, one came and said to him, "good teacher, what good thing shall I do that I may have eternal life? So he said to him, "Why do you call Me good? No one is good but one, that is, God. But if you want to enter into life, keep the commandments."

He said to him, "which ones? Jesus said, "You shall not murder, you shall not commit adultery, you shall not steal, you shall not bear false witness, honor your father and your mother, and you shall love your neighbor as yourself."

The young man said to him, all these things I have kept from my youth, what do I still lack? Jesus said to him, "If you want to be perfect go and sell what you have and give to the poor and you will have treasure in heaven and come and follow Me.".

When the young man had heard that saying he went away sorrowful for he had great possessions. Then Jesus said to his disciples, "Assuredly I say to you that it is hard for a rich man to enter the kingdom of heaven, and again I say to you it is easier for a camel to go through the eye of a needle than for a rich man to enter the kingdom of God.".

Notice that the young rich man was doing a lot of things right! Jesus did not rebuke him for any of them, so the young man was telling the truth.

There was one thing the young man had that was more important to him than Jesus. Riches! Jesus told him, "go sell all you have, give to the poor and you will have treasure in heaven." Jesus was not telling him go live in a tent and never have anything again. Jesus was telling him to get rid of the idol that you trust and value more than me and you will have an inheritance in heaven. Jesus wanted the young man to remove the one thing that came between him and Jesus. The young man walked away sorrowful; he refused to give up the one thing that became sin to him. Jesus wanted the young man to put riches in the right place in his life below Jesus and not above Jesus. The young man could possibly have riches again in the future depending on what Jesus call on the young mans life was., but now Jesus would be influencing the young man with his riches and decisions. Jesus would be God in his life not money. Then Jesus could be able to trust him with even more than he had to start with.

Remember Judas made that fatal error of putting money before Jesus and betrayed Jesus. Judas never confessed to Jesus his love of money. Jesus was waiting on Judas to confess, but Judas kept silent. That meant Judas didnt want to get rid of the covetousness of money. So all the time Judas was with Jesus, Money was his true god. Thats why he was capable of betraying Jesus. Satan had a home in Judas because Judas loved somthing of the world more than Jesus. Later at the last supper, scripture says Satan entered Judas. Jesus is not against riches, he is against covetousness. Judas is not in Heaven because he trusted a wrong god.

Rich people can do a lot of good to a lot of people. Look what Jesus said after the young man left.

Mark 10:26, 30

And they were astonished beyond measure saying among themselves, "Who then can be saved?" But looking at them, Jesus said, "With men it is impossible but not with God, for with God all things are possible." Then Peter began to say to Him, "See we have left all and followed you" So Jesus answered and said, "Assuredly I say to you that there is no one who has left house or brothers or sisters or father, or mother or wife or children or lands, for my sake and the gospels, who shall not receive a hundredfold now in this time, houses and brothers and sisters and mothers and children and lands with persecutions and in the age to come, eternal life.

When I got saved I began to see money differently. I began to trust money less and God more. He did some incredible financial things in my life. Work your skills and talents. Work is given by God. These things are Gods provision.

These are people who got their priorities right, and God added far more to them than they originally had to begin with. Riches must be in the right place in your life, and you will be blessed. Receiving the kingdom of God is receiving Jesus and His salvation into your heart. The kingdom of heaven is the physical place, heaven itself. You must have the kingdom of God in your heart to enter the kingdom of heaven. The young rich man in the story could not enter into the kingdom of God, meaning receiving Jesus as Lord.

He walked away from Jesus, sorrowful. Jesus did not refuse him; he refused Jesus. Giving what little you have in your life becomes a seed in Jesus that then multiplies, and in the end you have more than what you started with. Your faith is investing in Him. Die to self-will to reap a eternal glorious life.

God loves to bless his people, Abraham was rich, Isaac was rich, Jacob was rich, David was rich, Solomon was rich, Joseph became the second in command in Egypt, and he was rich. The list goes on. They were all workers. They were not rich because of greed but because they feared and honored God. God came first. Their faith was in God not the riches, and God blessed them.

[Deutereronomy 28: all the chapter] The first half begins "Now it shall come to pass that if you diligently obey the voice of the Lord your God, to observe carefully all His commandments which I command you today, that the Lord your God will set you high above the nations of the Earth". Then God lists the blessings.

In the second half of the chapter from verse 15 and on- it says, "But it shall come to pass that if you do not obey the voice of the Lord your God, to observe carefully all His commandments and His statutes which I command you today, that all these curses will come upon you and overtake you". Then he lists all the curses. It would be an eye opener to those who read this chapter.

Obedience brings blessing.

Jeremiah 29:11:

"For I know the thoughts that I think toward you, says the Lord, thoughts of peace and not of evil, to give you a future and a hope.

12 then you will call upon Me and go and pray to Me, and I will listen to you.

13 and you will seek Me and find Me, when you search for Me with all your heart. I will be found by you says the Lord and I will bring you back from your captivity; I will gather you from all the nations and from all the places I have driven you to the place from which I cause you to be carried away captive.

I hope and pray that this testimony will encourage you that there is no sin so deep that God will not forgive. No pain so deep that God cannot heal it. No self-worthlessness and condemnation that you think about yourself that God cannot pull you out of and set you high upon a rock of self-worth because you are the son or daughter of a king. Jesus gives you great worth and eternal life. Trust Him. He has great plans for your life. Find out what they are.

It is not how you start the race but how you finish. You are not locked into your past failures. Drop the past like a live hand grenade. The past robs from the future. When a runner looks back, it slows him down. I was not going to be a product of my past by focusing on it! Instead I grabbed ahold of the new life and goals Christ gave me. A new way of thinking. Becoming what I was created to be in the first place. Past pain is gone, and a future is ahead.

1 Peter 4:8: above all things have fervent love for one another, for "Love covers a multitude of sin."

Psalm 37; 4–5: Delight yourself in the Lord and He will give you the desires of your heart, commit your way to the Lord trust in Him and He shall bring it to pass.

Hosea 4:6 my people are destroyed for lack of knowledge.

Chapter 3

Now Salvation Begins

I was saved in July 1985. It was remarkable what started happening. I was twenty-five years old. In all the years I was going to a religious church, nothing like this ever happened to me before.

Matthew 6: 33: "But seek first the kingdom of God and his righteousness, and all these things shall be added unto you."

I was saved in my living room in July of 1985. I asked Jesus into my heart and to forgive me of my sins. The power of God, the Holy Spirit, came into me and I could feel it. I wasn't sure what was happening, but I felt the change and the power and the forgiveness. It was great. I could feel the physical manifestation in my heart. I was clean and saved and accepted by God. It felt so good . It was exciting. It only took a couple of minutes after I understood that I needed to receive Jesus.

The first thing that happened was I got an insatiable hunger for the word of God; just the first week. I was in the Bible four hours a day after I got home from work. I was amazed at the wisdom that was in it. It was the first time I ever desired to even read the Bible. The Holy Spirit was in me now and giving me the hunger to feed on the word. It's the same as a newborn baby: the first thing the baby wants is to eat, and they have an insatiable hunger. I was understanding it. Within one week after my salvation I was completely released from alcohol, beer on weekdays and hard booze on weekends. I took a drink of beer, and it tasted like drain cleaner! It was the last beer in my refrigerator. I took the rest and poured it down the drain and said "I don't need this anymore! I was completely free; it was like I never did it.

I just want to say this: if you're an alcoholic or a drug addict of any kind and in bondage to anything that you can't put down, Jesus can deliver you of it, no matter how long you have done it. Just receive him and believe and watch Him work. I was free in 1985 and have not touched alcohol again till this day. Thirty-four-plus years without touching a drop. It wasn't hard; it was like I never did it. Any kind of addiction, whether cocaine, heroin, sex, pornography, etc. are satanic strongholds designed to keep you in bondage and in continuous guilt so you always feel condemned. We are condemned already and more sin just intensifies the guilt we are already in. It is Satan's way of controlling us and possessing us.

What I realized over the years is that when we sin, we are feeling Satan's condemnation, Satan walked away from God Therefore disconnecting himself from all the virtues of God through rebellion. He became pure evil. [Isaiah 14:12,14] Then he got Adam to rebel and Eve decieved against God and they both became disconnected from God. Mankind became evil. Jesus has come to restore us to our position With God.

Death and sin and injustice have a root cause, our own rebellious flesh that operates in the natural: taste, feel or touch, hear, smell, or see. Our flesh operates in the physical world. It doesn't know spiritual matters. Satan tempts us to stay in our flesh natural man, to ignore the spiritual part, your heart, or conscience. God changes the human spirit with a new one, the Holy Spirit. Your motives then start to change to holy righteous motives instead of manipulative, hypocritical, self-serving ones.

We are internally not capable of saving ourselves. We need things from the outside of us to come into us just to live life. We need water, food, air, knowledge, and more that all comes from the outside and we have to take them inside of us to survive. Why should it surprise you that our spirit aka, heart needs an outside influence to come into us to save us. The Holy Spirit is in the Earth waiting to enter anybody who will accept Him. Your spirit is slowly wasting away as you get older without the infusion of the Holy Spirit to regenerate you.

There is a moth that doesnt eat. It is called the Hercules moth. Largest moth in the world but has no mouth. It lives 10 to 14 days only sustaining on what it ate as a catapillar. In other words it uses up only what was inside it with out any renewal. in short it burns out, using up what it had inside of it. That is one way to describe mankind without Jesus. No Spiritual renewal. At old age we burn out.

With Jesus, He regenerates our Spirit, aka, heart, that sustains us through death. Jesus puts a new life inside us that will be released when our flesh dies. We leave the body and are living a new life in Heaven. A seed breaks out of the outside shell and becomes a new life. We leave our bodys behind and become a new life. Without the Holy Spirit of Life infusion from Jesus, we are both dead outside and inside. The body dies and so does the soul in hell.

Without Christ- the body is left behind and the rest is thrown into the fire pile, hell.

John: 8:34–36: "Jesus answered them, 'Most assuredly, I say to you, whoever commits sin is a slave of sin, and a slave does not abide in the house forever. Therefore if the son makes you free, you shall be free indeed.'"

This is why holiness is so important, because it takes you from a condemned slave to a sinless son or daughter.

A slave wouldn't have a personal relationship with his master. They are told what to do in order to survive. A son or daughter does have a personal relationship with their father. They eat at his table because they are family.

God gave me a strong desire to witness to people wherever I went. Little did I know that there would be such resistance to it. I had found the treasure of life and couldn't wait to share it so other people could be free too. I had escaped death and found Christ, who had gave me eternal life, and I couldn't wait for others to get Him too.

I started with my family naturally and people at work. All these people knew me before I was saved. The guys at work said, boy has he changed! They saw what a jerk I was and heartless before and now all of a sudden within a couple of days I was changed.

My family had the biggest hard time with it because we were all raised Catholic and anything else to them was just a cult in their way of thinking. But what happened to me was a living intervention of Jesus right in my living room. It was real! They could not see that, and my dad especially was bothered.

He said I was acting better than everybody else. But that wasn't true. I was telling them about being saved and how God loves them and he was getting convicted about his own sin. It was bringing conviction of his own sin to the surface.

That is what the presence of God will do to a person: first, it will bring conviction so that they will turn to Christ and get their sin forgiven and get saved. This is why John the Baptist came first before Jesus. He was anointed by God and called to call men to repentance, to not only prepare the way, but to give people a place to confess their sin and come clean about their sin. It says in scripture that John was baptizing them, and they were confessing their sins. Then John steered them next toward Jesus. You must see your need for a Savior. If you are able to see your sin then you are able to see your need for a Savior.

You must be truthful about yourself and truthful with God to receive the spirit of truth, the Holy Spirit. He does not turn away those who will come to Him.

Mark 2:17: When Jesus heard it He said to them, "Those who are well have no need of a physician, but those who are sick. I did not call the righteous, but sinners to repentance."

The only problem is that there is no righteous people on the earth. They are self-proclaimed righteous. Jesus is telling them that there is nothing He can do for them unless they come to the point of getting rid of their self-righteousness and seeing and confessing their sin and their need for Jesus and salvation. [Romans 10:3,4] Everyone in the whole world is sick and sinful until they come to Christ. Every human on earth needs Jesus for eternal life and an abundant life in this life. Self-righteousness is not reality! We will not withstand the judgment claiming our own righteousness. Even we Christians when we do what's right give glory to God and not to ourselves. It is His spirit working in us to do right.

[Romans 10:3,4] says "For they being ignorant of Gods righteousness, and going about to establish their own righteousness, not having submitted themselves unto the righteousness of God. For Christ is the end of the law to righteousness to every one who believes."

[Romans 3:10, 12] As it is written; "There is none righteous, no not one; there is none who understands; there is none who seeks after God. They have all gone out of the way; they have together become unprofitable; there is none who does good, no, not one."

Do not blame anyone else; just come to Jesus by faith and be saved. Live above sin, God will give you the strength you need. He doesn't expect you to do it yourself because you can't. He has placed goals and dreams in your heart that he wants to accomplish in you. It will take faith in him to accomplish them.

As I was witnessing to my family, one day I was showing my dad in the Bible where Mary the mother of Jesus had other kids after Jesus was born. He didn't believe it. The Catholics consider her a deity. I showed him in the Bible that they had at their house. My dad looked at me and said that if you tell any of your brothers and sisters I will kill you! Well I told him, you're never touching me again! And I walked out of the house. I never did stop talking to them either. I was learning that persecution comes with having

Christ in me. People were getting convicted about their sin and didn't seem to want to get rid of it. So the natural thing for them to do was to resist me, blame me, and say that I went off the deep end. Shoot the messenger and the message is dead. Wrong!!! God's word will live through eternity when this age is long gone. Focusing on the messenger does no good because the message is living and backed by God and cannot be destroyed. He has more messengers.

Satan lost one of his prime servants when he lost me! I was getting falling dreams that were trying to kill me in my sleep. Once in a while I had some affliction in my body that I had to stand in faith for to be healed. And eventually I get healed. Satan didn't leave without a fight. But now the fight was not in my spirit but in just my flesh and my soul. Jesus had my heart. They eventually began to subside as I was resisting the devil and he must flee (James 4:7).

As I was in the word, God began to speak to my heart and give me revelation, which means the word went from my mind and into my heart. Then I was able to start believing God for the supernatural. I was talking to a guy at work, Brian, about Jesus and he was a Catholic. He had a lot of questions, and over the months we would talk but he never came over to salvation because of the stronghold of religion. One day we were clocking in for work in the morning, and he came up to me and said I have to tell you something! It was urgent.

Now Brian loved his mom. She was dead for some years, and it was still tearing him up to this day. He said that as he was sleeping last night, his mom came into his bed room. It woke him up suddenly. She came and sat on the bed, and there was weight on the bed. She looked good and was dressed nice and smiling.

Brain's guard was down then. She said to him something like, "Brian, you know how close you and I are and how much I love you, but you can't listen to Marty and his pastor and what they are telling you." Then she disappeared. This was a manifested angel of light. Necromancy, consulting the dead on behalf of the living. A demon taking the shape of his mother to get in close to him to get him to not listen to the word I was giving him to be saved. Brian was petrified. I hadn't gave up on Brian, and obviously demons were trying to stop him from ever believing by using the closest person to him. Beware that as you hear this message to be saved that you don't let anyone steal it from you. People close to you can be used to keep you from it. Dont wait for anyone else even if your married and your spouse doesnt agree. Save yourself and then you can help save others. The seed you sow today can grow into salvation tomorrow in someone's life. I did not receive Christ the first time I ever heard of a born-again Christian. I thought it was weird.

Another person at work wanted me to come to his house sometimes and talk to him about salvation. I went one Saturday in the afternoon and gave him the gospel and prayed with him. He got saved right in his living room. He was carrying a lot of guilt in his life because his past. He was driving one day, I believe drunk, and got into an accident and his wife was killed. He was raising his two daughters by himself, and a day didn't go by without it tormenting him. I believe Jesus lifted that off of him. He was excited that he was forgiven. This man was serious about Jesus. He had gotten to a place that he knew he needed Him. When he heard the gospel, he without hesitation received it and was saved. Jesus is looking for those who are hungry for Him.

In contrast, Brian, who I mentioned earlier was not ready. He did not believe but resisted. He didn't want to let go of his sin. One of the many reasons was his religious, traditional up bringing that he had. He never saw the power of God or saw him intervene in his life. Those who are religious believe in their mind there is a God but do not believe with the heart. Belief is not in the head but in the heart! In the head only opposes the power of God. Those who are religious like to talk the talk but stop short of receiving Christ and letting the power of God move in their lives. God wants your heart, not just your head, aka soul. So many people just believe if they mentally believe in God that it is enough.

Ask yourself; do you believe in God but your heart is not for God? Or your heart is somewhere else? Then you still need to get saved. Revelation 3:20 says Jesus knocks on the door of your heart, not your mind. True belief is in the heart!

Many just don't understand because they are not taught it. The Pharisees that apposed Jesus were hypocrites. Their hearts were not for God, just their minds. They knew the laws of God better than the people. That is why they killed Jesus so it didn't expose them. Pharisees were in it for the money and public honor. Pharisees are in world churches today, but they have no power because the leadership doesnt submit to the moving of the spirit of God. Then the buck stops with them and not Jesus, they stay in control. They give a soft message, leaving out parts they believe will offend people because they want your money and your attendance. These churches keep the people through entertainment. So these pastors are then Idoliters that God cannot move through. The church stays sick with sin.

So the people are not given the whole council of God and left to die on the vine. These pastors and ministers who do this are a stench in the nostriles of God!

My daughter and me were invited to a church for a christmas program. Her co-worker said it was the best church, very spiritual. She talked me into going on Sunday morning. The singers and musicians were vey good. The pastor said nice things. We sat in the very back. I noticed such apathy in the people. My daughter went back to work and her co-worker asked how she liked it. She asked him, does your church preach against sin and about holiness and righteousness? He said oh no no! if they did that, everyone would leave.

[John 4:24] "God is Spirit and those who worship Him must worship Him in spirit and in truth."

[truth includes;] You cannot worship God with sin stained hands. If you are not saved and going to church, your worship is in vain. If you are saved, make sure that any sin you are doing or practicing is confessed to Jesus and put under His blood. truth means you are honest with God. Be real. As you walk with Jesus, sin gets weaker and righteousness gets stronger. If you dont have Christ, BE HONEST and ask Him in your life. This is truth. You can go to a Spirit filled church to be saved and delivered. You can get saved in your own house like I did.

Another reason people don't come to Christ is that they enjoy their sin and don't want to give it up but act like they do, so it is heartless religion. Not real! God cannot be fooled. You need to realize that Jesus will deliver you of sin, so it doesn't have to be a great wrestling match and a struggle.

Why is it so important to get rid of sin? Sin came into the world through Satan. Satan is eternally condemned. Those who practice sin like him will be condemned with him. Sin cannot enter heaven or God's presence. God's holiness would destroy that person the moment he came near. That is why the change must happen on earth now with Jesus before you go to heaven, so you can stand in the presence of God. Jesus and his blood sacrifice erases the sin and gives you holiness.

It is dangerous to hear the gospel and not receive it right away, but God has mercy and is longsuffering and is not willing that any should perish. Tomorrow is never guaranteed to us. As I talked to people at work about Jesus I was quickly getting a reputation at work. It started dividing me and my brothers and parents. They were starting to call me preacher man at work. I talked to a lot of guys. You could tell that some thought about it and had questions. Pete was a Christian at the plant who talked to me about salvation shortly before I got saved. I want to give him honor in this book. Things were happening all the time. At work, I was stirring up the conviction in these people. I was talking to anybody who would listen.

One day one of the bullies at the plant who weighed about 250 lbs. was intimidating a small guy who was a friend of mine over by the pop machines. He was standing over him like a big repulsive ape, saying all kinds of unmentionable things to him. He had a big mouth, and this guy Bill was someone I had real mercy for because you could see he was beat down in life. Now I weighed about 225 lbs., and when I saw this, my anger rose up in me. I said "why don't you pick on someone your own size"! He is twice as small as you! He said to me "what are you going to do about it?" And as he walked up to me I said, "Whatever is necessary" He looked at me and mumbled and walked away. I was not sure I could take him, but I could not watch that any more. God saw to it that the bully got a fear of me in him later on. He never messed with me, and even later on through time I worked with this guy and we got along well, and he and I had real respect. I wanted him to see the light of Jesus in me, and I completely forgave him and held no grudge at all. All have sinned and come short of the glory of God.

People at work who mocked me behind my back would not say anything to my face unless they were in a group. One time I left my work station and came back a little later, and there was a note in my work area that was lying there. It said "Jesus loves you but everyone else here thinks you're an @#$%$#" so Satan went to work on my mind right away and said see everybody here hates you! Then God said to me right after that "Marty, one man put that note in your work station, it's not everybody" I said yeah, yeah, that's right, and suddenly I felt strength go into me, and I was encouraged by God. I had joy after that. Then God gave me a word of knowledge and told me who put the note in my work area. He did this to see how I would handle it, if I would forgive and hold no bitterness or not, but notice that it was after he encouraged me. So it was no problem to forgive, and I treated him with kindness even after the incident.

We do have to discern people though, such as, to realize whether they are dangerous or friendly or are honest or a liar or a thief. This keeps us from harm's way, but judgment and punishment or whether someone is going to hell or heaven is God's place. The police and court systems and prisons are designed by God to take dangerous people off the streets. Prisoners can get saved in prison and get a second chance. Murderers and rapists can all get saved and be forgiven.

Look at Matthew 5:25–26 and Romans 13:4: Anyone not believing in Jesus will eventually end up in eternal prison and torture called the lake of fire any way.

Read Romans 4:14, "It is before God we stand or fall, not mankind.

You must remember that any attack from an unbeliever on christan, if he or she doesn't get saved will give an account to God for that persecution. I had to forgive people not only for their sake, but for mine, so that I was not controlled by that person. My mind will not be preoccupied with it. Satan likes to cause unforgiveness because your mind will be preoccupied with that person and not on the word of God and can cause a crippling effect on your faith and eventually cause bitterness that spreads to every part of your life if given time. Because the mind and the heart will not be in unity together to let faith work. Your spirit will be telling you one thing, your soul another. Jesus said you must forgive from the heart. Leave the judgment of people to the righteous judge Jesus.

The people I was talking to, or friends with, were potential believers. They were getting picked on by other workers. So I would encourage them, and one in particular was John. Two guys would go to his work station and mouth off to him and mock him; it was the devil in these two, and John didn't have the Holy Spirit to fight off attacks like this. John wasn't saved yet. I prayed for Johns protection against these guys as he told me about it. Then not long after that, one of them got hit by a power sweeper and wound up in the hospital with surgerys for six months. His friend who picked on John was alone now.

I caught him in the bathroom one day. I said to him where's your buddy? "See what happens to people who mock the word of God"? He didn't say anything at all. But he did go and tell his friend what I said, I'm sure of it, because when this guy who got hurt finally came back to work after he was healed, he simmered down and didn't say anything to me for a long while. But one day he walked up to me and said that he didn't know what the heck he was, whether saved or lost or what condition he was in with God.

That sweeper injury made him think. He knew God was getting his attention or he wouldn't have come and talked to me about salvation.

I knew he wasn't saved. So I talked to him about Jesus and his mercy on him, just being a light and waiting for whosoever would want to know about salvation. Jesus said forgive 70 times 7. One of the points I am making out of this is God fights battles far better than we can. But we have to give the battle to Him first. He is a living God and has power to judge. He has given the believer authority on earth over demons. Demons work through people. Demons moving around without bodies scare people. We call them ghosts. And I have seen them. But demons that are working in a human are dangerous because they can cause physical harm and physically carry out their wicked plans. When you see things like mass shootings, this is a demon or demons carrying out the act that the human has let into his life. Demons have no virtue, no heart, no compassion, and no mercy. They hate God and people. Jesus said that Satan comes to steal, kill, and destroy.

God has no vulnerability, no weakness. Satan cannot defeat God at all! So Satan goes after the people that God loves in order to get to God. So God sent Jesus to make us children of God so God could legally intervene in our lives and defeat Satan through Jesus living in us by the Holy Spirit, and give us eternal life and take our place in the heavens. Satan's food and delight is the death and destruction of humans.

Romans 13:19–21:

"Beloved do not avenge yourselves, but rather give place to wrath; for it is written, vengeance is mine, I will repay says the Lord.

20: therefore, if your enemy hungers feed him; if he thirsts, give him a drink; for so in doing you heap coals of fire on his head.

21: do not be overcome with evil but overcome evil with good ."

Overcoming evil with good starts with overcoming the evil of our own life and saying no! Then you can begin to resist the evil in other people with good. Resist evil in yourself first, then you will see straight to see and recognise the evil in others. through Jesus, who will give you the victory.

Meanwhile back in my private life things were getting exciting. God was filling me with the word, and Satan was fighting me tooth and nail in my thought life, my mind. To try to discredit God on my new birth and create as much doubt as he could while I was still young in the Lord. Trying to make me believe that God didn't care. He does his destructive deeds in a person's life, then whispers in my ear that God is mad at you and you are being punished, which is an outright lie. God came to give us life and that more abundantly, and Satan comes to steal, kill, and destroy. His tactics were not working, because the next thing that happened was my stolen all-terrain vehicle or ATV.

I was saved probably less than a month and excited about my walk with the Lord. I was getting ready for work one morning. I had to be into work by 5:00 a.m. so at about 4:30 in the morning I walked outside to find my locked garage door wide open, and my Honda 200 x all-terrain motorcycle was stolen out of the garage. These were all ATV 3 wheelers. I had three of them in the garage at the time. One was in the middle of repair and the other was a small one, a Honda 125 cc. I checked the garage and saw that the 200x was gone. I didn't really get mad because I knew right away that Satan had put it in someone's heart to steal it to get to me and produce doubt in my heart about God. I knew better but wondered a little. This ATV was worth $2,500 dollars.

So right there in my backyard in the dark at 4:30 in the morning I shouted, "Satan! You're not going to get to me this way. God I thank you for getting my ATV back; it's not yet totally paid for. and I ask you to help me get it back!" I felt doubt but stayed with my confession.

I called the police and filed a report and showed the title. So it was registered with the police.

I had no idea how I was going to get my ATV back. I went to work and I told my brother who was working at the same place at that time, and he said he would help me find it. But I had no idea where to even start looking.

We lived in the city, the Fox Cities: Oshkosh, Neenah, Menasha, and Appleton, all pretty much tied together. This was truly a needle in a haystack with easily 40,000-plus people; who knows? But God was at work the minute I prayed and gave it to Him that morning. I got home that night, the same day it happened, and before I could get in the house a woman came up to me and said "did someone steal an ATV out of your garage this morning"? I said yes! She said, "I think I know who has got it!" She said that they run a halfway house on the other side of the block and there was a guy put there by the court. He saw me riding my ATV in the back yard with my son and began a plot to steal it and run away from the halfway house. He tried to get others to go with him, but they wouldn't. Turns out that this guy was originally from Oshkosh, the city next door. I thanked her greatly, and I thanked God for his hand moving on this situation. He let me know what city to look in.

So I told my brother about it. I am condensing this story; the whole thing played out for about a little over two weeks. My brother and I started searching trails in Oshkosh all over the city. I kept stopping at the Oshkosh police station every so often to see if anything was reported. They always said no. A week went by, and my brother had to do other stuff, but I was grateful for his help in the searching. So I kept going every day I could take some time. I knew that time was of the utmost importance if I wanted to find it in one piece. Usually they are found in the woods somewhere, destroyed, or you don't see them ever again. So finally the next Saturday came that I could take some time to drive to Oshkosh and look again. I wasn't even taking my other ATV any more to go on trails. I was starting to give up, so I was just driving around by trails and fields to see what I could see. It's already past two weeks since the ATV was stolen, and I had serious doubts about finding it.

I said to God, doubting, "You don't want me to find this thing, do you?" It was Saturday, and I had already decided this was going to be my last day of looking. There was no evidence anywhere or anybody anywhere who said that they see anything. So I was at a stop sign in Oshkosh getting ready to head home and all of a sudden God spoke to my spirit and said, "go to the motor cycle shop out towards the prison and talk to the man at the shop." He showed me in my memory the motorcycle shop, which I had seen before.

So I obeyed the voice and went to the cycle shop like He told me. I went inside and talked to the guy behind the counter. I asked him if he knew anywhere where people can ride off road dirt bikes or ATVs. He said yes. They are riding out on some trails by the new prison. I told him thank you and left for the prison. The prison was a new place that gave a tour to the public before it was opened. We took that tour, so I knew where the prison was. So as I was driving out on the country roads by the prison, I got to a stop sign. I remember thinking, I'm going home!

Then I looked to my right, and down the road about a half mile down, I saw four guys standing around an ATV with a flat tire. So I got interested. I drove down there thinking if it wasn't mine, maybe they saw mine somewhere. So as I got closer, it looked more and more like my ATV. And as I pulled up I saw where there were two scratches I put on the gas tank, and I knew instantly it was my ATV.

So I pulled in real close to block them from running off with it. God was with me, and I got the victory! As I pulled up, the guy who stole it said "this is my ATV! I've had it for six months." I hadn't even stopped or said anything yet but my window was open, and he was scared. This guy was bigger than me. My adrenalin was surging. I got fixated and tuned everything out and climbed out of the van to go after him, but in my zeal I neglected to put the van in park. Whoops! So when I climbed out, my van took off without me. The other guys that were there shouted "your van" I looked, I chased it down the road and it stopped next to a farm field, I was able to catch it without damage. Now I'm really wound up. I went back to them and punched the guy right between the eyes.

Then I told those other guys what he did, and how he got it out of my garage. They were his friends. Then I punched him again. Then I told him you better turn yourself in. The police are looking for you. The other guys were very willing to help me load up the ATV in my van so I wouldn't turn them in. I forgave the guy in my heart, but he did do about 125.00 dollars' worth of damage to it and partly bent one of the axles. Other than that it was okay. To God be the glory for showing me where to go to find it. Please note that God didn't throw it in my lap. I had to do my part by faith and be diligent to look for it. Keep believing, even though doubt was creeping in. The police picked him up later, I heard.

I told my brother about it as soon as I could. He couldn't believe it. He knew the odds were next to impossible. My brother is an unbeliever. He has never accepted Jesus Christ. So I told him, look what God can do. I told him how God spoke to me at the stop sign to go to the motorcycle shop, but he didn't believe it. So the next thing that happened probably within a week of me finding my ATV, my brother's ATV got stolen out of his garage—no kidding; I couldn't make this stuff up. He called me up and told me what happened. His garage was open and his Honda 250 ATV was stolen. He had no clue where to even begin looking. He lived in the Fox Cities also, with thousands of people, another needle in a haystack. So I said to him, "if God can get my bike back, he can get yours back"! So I said to him," will you let me pray for you to get it back?"

He said okay. So I said "God, you got my ATV back for me, and now I ask that you would have mercy on my brother and help him to get his ATV back, and I thank you in Jesus name amen."

He said thanks but didn't really believe it but I did. Because we had no idea where to look for the ATV, we didn't go anywhere to start looking. I got a call about four days later from my brother; he was excited. He said that he found his ATV. "Wow, where was it?" I asked. He said that he took his little son down to the railroad tracks behind the house to catch butterflies, and as they were there he noticed matted-down grass that was in three ruts. So he followed them down to a house on the same block to a shed. He looked inside the crack in the door and saw his all-terrain vehicle, so he took it, and his son's skate board was there too. He called the police, and they took the report. My brother got to see the hand of God move, even though he wasn't a believer. I wish I could say that he got saved but he didn't.

The odds are astronomical in the cities we lived in to find both ATVs intact with thousands of people and residents.

To finish this testimony, after I was saved and was meeting other Christians, I actually met the guy who stole the ATV out of my brother's garage. He was from Minnesota. He wasn't saved back then, and he got done partying one night and saw the ATV in my brother's garage and stole it to take back to Minnesota to buy drugs with. But for some reason he got disinterested in it and left it there. That was the move of God. No one got in trouble with the police. God took care of it all. This guy got saved later on. Glory to God.

As I was walking with the Lord I was getting stronger in the spirit, and I was on the praise team at our church playing bass guitar. God was showing me about moving more in faith, but I wasn't seeing that attitude at the Assembly of God we were going to. It was dead, and there was a lot of unbelief. They had prayer lines, but we never heard any testimonies about people getting healed. We loved the people there but it was apathetic. People get comfortable in their churches and don't press forward to new things God wants to do. Religion does not really believe God will move but will go through the motions. It was getting unbearable. We would let traveling ministers put their campers at our house and an evangelist stayed with us one time and went to our church on Sunday just to attend, not to preach. I was still learning, and I asked him what do you see wrong with our church that there is no power of God moving? He said it's religion. I didn't quite get it, but it started to open my eyes to man's efforts and apathy and unbelief to a world of faith and wanting God's power to move.

A friend of ours felt the same way and was checking out new churches and found one in the city that had some faith and told us about it. It was a Word church. We didn't know anything about these churches. We went one night and liked what we saw. The pastor was moving in the gift of words of knowledge and tongues and interpretation (1 Cor. 12:8–10). We found a church that God was able to move among his people because there was faith there to receive. The pastor was submitted to God. We were on the praise team there, and I became an elder.

We stayed there and made some good friends. God was putting things for me to do in front of me. One day I was at my parents' house, and they asked me if I had seen the newspaper. No, I said. They gave me the paper and showed me the article. Ed, who was a bartender at the biker bar that I was a DJ at years ago was in a motorcycle crash. The paper said he was going over the bridge with no helmet on and was speeding at night and could not make the off ramp and went head over heels into a valley. He had brain damage, and the article said he was in critical condition. Just then God said to me," go up to the hospital and pray for Ed." I didn't say anything to my family about it and left the house later.

I was scared to go up to the hospital to pray for Ed. I had never done anything like that before. I was resisting God and reasoning with him that they wouldn't let me near him unless I was a family member or relative. This went on for two weeks. God wouldn't let up on me about it. So I asked a member of our church to go with me. We picked a night and went up to the hospital.

When we got to Ed's floor, we went to the nurses station and asked about Ed. They said he will die or remain the way he is. Turns out that he was straight across from the nurses station. I asked, "Could we go see him? I am an old friend. They said sure. That was a relief. So we went in there and saw Ed hooked up to all kinds of machines and a tracheostomy in his throat. About two weeks had passed already, and there has been no changes.

I had my Bible with me. I said to Ed, "Ed, God has sent us up here to pray for you, and we believe you are going to be healed and come out of this bed. Ed was not moving at all. His flesh is damaged, but I was speaking to his spirit. We are made of three parts: spirit, soul, and body; his spirit was still okay.

I opened up the Bible to Isaiah 53:5: "But He was wounded for our transgressions, he was bruised for our iniquities; the chastisement for our peace was upon him, and by his stripes we are healed."

I continued with 1 Peter 2:24: who Himself bore our sins in his own body on the tree, that we having died to sins, might live for righteousness- by whose stripes you were healed.

I prayed in tongues for a bit, and Ed's hand started moving. All of a sudden there was a guy behind a curtain that we didn't even know was there and he started making noise. Things were happening. I finished praying, and as we were leaving I said to Ed "we did what God told us to do; now it's up to the Lord. We will see you later." I waited two days, and on the second day I called up to the hospital and asked the nurse, "How is Ed doing? She said he improved 100 percent. He came out of the coma. Praise God. Later on maybe a week later I went up to the hospital to see Ed. He was off the machines and in a different room watching tv. I walked in, and he was excited to see me. He reached out to me, and I gave him a hug. He could not speak yet and he was moving slow. He was in a wheelchair. I talked to him what I could and then left. A year or two later we saw him at a beach with some friends, not really talking and still in a wheelchair but he was a long way from being dead.

Just a note on the mercy of God. The last time I saw Ed, he was a bartender who knew nothing about salvation. Judging from this accident and the circumstances of it that I won't go into, Ed still knew nothing of salvation, but God had mercy on him.

By this time I was getting dreams, a lot of them from God. Joel:2: 28–29 says, "And it shall come to pass afterward that I will pour out my spirit on all flesh; your sons and your daughters shall prophecy, your old men shall dream dreams, and your young men shall see visions; and also on my men servants and on my maid servants I will pour out my spirit in those days.

[Dream] God showed me in a dream that I was standing with a multitude of people in a place, and there was a raised platform in front of us. Then I saw Jesus on the platform pointing to different people in the crowd. I couldn't see His face, but he was dressed in white with a gold sash around his chest. As He was pointing, he was going across the crowd, and he pointed to me and then kept going. Not everyone was picked. The scripture He gave me for this dream was Matthew 22:14: "For many are called but few are chosen." I was called to minister.

In Matthew 22:2, 9 this parable that Jesus taught. A king arranged a marriage for his son and sent out servants to call those who were invited to the wedding; and they were not willing to come. Again he sent out other servants saying, "I have prepared my dinner my oxen and my fatted cattle are killed, and all things are ready, come to the wedding But they made light of it and went there ways, one to his own farm and another to his business. And the rest seized his servants treated them spitefully and killed them. But when the king heard about it he was furious.

And he sent out his armies, and destroyed those murderers, and burned up there city. Then he said to his servants, the wedding is ready, but those who were invited were not worthy therefore go into the highways and as many as you find invite to the wedding."

Matthew 22:14 says, "Many are called but few are chosen." The common denominator of all these people who refused the supper was they had their eyes on something of this world that they gave more value than God. Notice too that these seemingly common people were capable of killing also. Their love for the world instead keeps them under Satan's authority; therefore, they were even capable of killing innocent people because Satan is a murderer! You need Jesus first. Things of the earth come second. God doesn't mind if you're a millionaire; you could be a help to many people. Just don't put your riches before Him. Remember, eternal life is only in Jesus! If He is not your Lord first in your life, then you do not have eternal life.

For example; if money is your god that comes before Jesus; that means it's the god of your heart! This means you believe in money! There is no eternal life in money. It is a man made thing that only does you any service on earth. So when you die, that god, money, will not get you into heaven. There is no eternal life in money! This goes for anything of this earth that is first in your life besides Jesus. He is the only one that can provide eternal life. Make the things of earth secondary and Jesus first, and you will be fine.

Jesus is the bride groom; we the believers are the bride; the wedding is being prepared for. If you do not want to come to the wedding, you are not His.

Jesus is called the second Adam. The first Adam failed! We are his bride, the second Eve! The first Eve failed. God is giving us back the earth and eternal life that we lost in the fall in the garden. We will rule with Christ.

Ask yourself, then, if I am not letting my life be fashioned into the likeness of Christ, then what is my life supposed to look like? Any belief system you put together yourself and live by will only be destroyed.

God calls many, but few really follow Him. When the people refused to come to the supper, they refused the king himself. This is not done in kingdoms where the king has absolute authority. The only way a person can be declared disobedient is if the person or law they refuse to listen to has authority over them or authority to tell them. If a stranger comes to you and tells you to do something, it's not disobedience to not do it, because they have no authority to tell you. They must ask you. But a king or, in this case, God himself, has authority to tell us, His creation, to repent and come to Christ or you will not see eternal life. Condemned.

Isaiah 45:12 says, I have made the earth and created man on it. I my hands stretched out the heavens, and all their host I have commanded.

What they did by refusing the king is refused to recognize his authority; they refused his kindness, refused his love, refused his sustaining of them to continue in peaceful lives. They rejected his eternal life he would have given them if they would have come to the supper and given him glory. In this case the king gave them life and can also take it away! It was absolutely evil and stupid to reject the king. Yet millions do today when God Himself the king made you and put you on the earth to begin with.

By the king inviting them and the people refusing, this showed what was in their hearts. They loved the world more than God and were destroyed.

As I said before, I was getting rejected by family concerning salvation and the message. They started to not have anything to do with me. When I was coming over to visit, they were putting the kids in the bedroom to play and telling them not to come out until I was gone because of the message I was preaching. It scared them! They wouldn't believe it. The spirit of God was present with me, and it convicted them.

Just a note: we did a lot together as a family—hunted together, fished together, and had family picnics together, especially my brothers and me. There is a real spiritual war that goes on between the unsaved and the saved. That brings me to the next dream I want to talk about.

[DREAM] About 1988 I had a dream one night that I was in a commercial bathroom, some bathroom at a business where there were stalls and so on.

I remember the layout of the bathroom exactly and where I was standing. I was standing in front of the mirror in the dream, and all of a sudden I saw my younger brother come out of the stall, and I hadn't seen him in about two years. And I said, Danny! And he said, Marty! We were happy to see each other. He walked toward me, and we hugged. I was really happy to see him, and he started wrestling me as we were hugging, trying to get me down to the ground. I wrestled back in self-defense; his hug was false. So as I wrestled him, I got him down and beat him. That was the end of the dream.

About six months later my family and I were at a Menards home improvement store. I was in the bathroom, and all of a sudden my brother came out of a stall. I was standing by the mirror. I looked and saw that it was the same stall that I saw in the dream. The whole bathroom was exactly how it looked in the dream. He came out of the stall, and he said Marty! I said Danny! Then I said, "I saw this in a dream, but he didn't understand. We hugged and talked, but of course we didn't wrestle, but it wasn't over yet.

We walked out into the store and kept talking, then the wrestling match started. He said to me "all I want is the old Marty back, and don't talk about God. I told him we can fish together but I will talk about God; He is my life now. How is it that you can talk about what you want but I cannot talk about what I want? Then I said to him "there is coming a time that the government is going to want to put a scanning code under your skin, then I showed him the UPC bar code on a package. I said "I don't know how they are going to do it, but they will find a way, then what will you do when you're not prepared?

This was in about 1989, before the RFID chip was public, so the only thing I could point to was the bar code on a package. He walked away sad and not saying a thing. The wrestling match was me getting emotional about my fellowship with my brother and shutting my mouth and denying Jesus who had just saved me. We could have gone fishing together easily, and he would have talked about whatever he wanted, but he was going to control my speech and stop me from talking about what I wanted to talk about. I won the wrestling match!!! Praise God, He showed me ahead of time. I hadn't seen my brother in over two years.

Jesus said in Luke 9: 61–62, And another said also, "Lord I will follow you, but let me first go and bid them farewell who are in my house." but Jesus said to him, "No one having put his hand to the plow, and looking back, is fit for the kingdom of God."

Whoever reads this book needs to understand that there is coming a time that Jesus will reign on this earth and the whole world will be filled with His glory. He will rule the earth, so make peace with Him now to get ready. Read your bible and see.

Habakkuk 2:14 says, For the earth will be filled with the knowledge of the glory of the Lord, as the waters cover the sea.

Jesus can be your Savior now or your judge later. He died for you; He would rather be your Savior. He wants us to judge ourselves and we would not be judged, and then we will see our need for Him. [1 Corinthians 11:31] says, if we would judge ourselves we would not be judged.

One day I was at work in my work station at the foundry. I was using air tools, a grinder, a cutting wheel, and other tools, grinding on iron castings, getting them ready for machining, a very noisy atmosphere. I had ear protection on and safety equipment. It was in this atmosphere that God came to me in a different way than before. I suddenly felt the presence of God so strong that I had to stop my tools. I felt His love like a cloud that enveloped me. It was so strong that I started getting emotional.

He said to me, to my spirit, "I want you to go and pray for the sick on Saturday at the hospital." I said okay, I will go. He showed me the hospital He wanted me to go to. There were three major ones in the Fox Cities. The one He showed me was the second farthest from where I lived. So as I said yes. I knew what I was saying, because, this Saturday was the beginning of deer season in Wisconsin, and I never missed opening weekend. This meant that I was going to miss opening day.

I couldn't tell God no. So after I said yes, that enveloping presence left me, and I was back to normal. Then reality really set in, and I realized that I was not going hunting Saturday. I knew it was God, and I was not going back on my word to Him as hard as it was. I went home and told my wife. She said "that's opening day of deer season!" I know I said but I told God I would go. This was Thursday morning that it happened.

So we got a babysitter on Saturday and proceeded to go to Saint Elizabeth's Hospital like God had showed me. As we were in the parking lot at the hospital, we prayed for a while before we went in. So we went inside not knowing where to go at all, or who to talk to. We knew no one up there. So I felt led to go to the second floor first. We went up there and were walking the halls, asking God, who do you want to talk to? There was this woman about twenty-five years old sitting in a bed with her door open, so I said "hey we're up here praying for the sick, can we pray for you? She got real scared and said no, no, no, I have a pastor who prays for me. Her wrists were both taped up. If she had slit her wrists that demon who caused her to do that sure didn't want to leave. She was not willing, so we left her alone. So next I felt God was saying go to the fourth floor.

So we went up to the fourth floor and started walking the halls. As we were walking, there was a door open and a woman about age twenty-five with a neck brace was sitting in bed and watching tv. I said to her, "hey we're up here praying for the sick, can we pray for you? She said sure, come on in real enthusiastically. I thought, well, God, this must be it. So we sat down and I began to tell her what had happened, how God told me to come up here three days ago.

She asked if I knew her mom and if her mom sent us up there.

I said no! I don't know your mom. God sent me up here. So I gave her the gospel message and reassured her of God's love for her. And we talked for a while. She started crying saying, saying "this is God! This is God! This is God!" She said she knew she needed to get right with God. It was a good meeting; she was crying. Before we left, she let us pray for her. I prayed for a husband for her and a quick healing in her neck. She got hurt in a baseball game and had to have surgery. We exchanged phone numbers and then we left. I was satisfied in my spirit that we had accomplished everything we were supposed to do. So we went home.

That same night, about 8.00 p.m. on the same day we were at the hospital, I got a call. Phone rings. Hello? The voice on the other end said, "who is this?" She didn't even say hello.

I said, "Marty." She then asked me, "Did you go up to the hospital today and pray for a young lady?" I said yes. Then I told her how God had talked to me three days ago and sent me up there and what happened at work. She was so grateful. She said "I am her mother. Me and Four other ladies from the Assembly of God church have been praying for her for four years. God told me three nights ago that he was sending help." That was the same day that

God approached me with His request at work. Praise God. Then she said," I don't know why I am telling you this, but my daughter is a lesbian." I said "Well, God can deliver her. She thanked me and that was the end of it. We never saw the woman again.

This woman needed to know God loved her outside of her mom telling her. She was feeling the condemnation of sin in her life style. And God in his mercy, by those woman praying for her, answering their prayers by sending someone up there with the salvation message in a way that the daughter could believe it was really God. God loves the sinners, but because he loves them, he will not leave them in their sinful condition. It will destroy you. Her heart was ready. Remember the other woman we wanted to pray for on the second floor? She wasn't ready. She needed salvation like this woman on the fourth floor but did not have a heart to repent and receive God's love. You must get to a place that you see your need for Jesus. You always did need Him right from the start, but it takes a lot of us going through some hardships in life to humble ourselves before God. It takes humility to ask for his help! He does not condemn you. Christ knows our condition and wants to save us.

I was getting a lot of dreams, and some really good things were happening. During all this I was going to a Super America gas station down the road from us. It was my favorite gas and grocery. I went there for years. During Desert Storm in about 1990 or so I was going to that station, and there was a woman there who was there almost full time at the cash register. So I got to talking to her about the Lord over time. We would talk about the war and current events, and I would always go back to the gospel and the end times we were in. She was willing to talk about the gospel and the war; I was kind of surprised that she liked talking about the war. Most woman I knew didn't really seem to take interest in things like that. So this went on for almost a year. One night I went to the station late and got gas, and it was slow, so that woman was outside working on the hand brake of her motorcycle because there were no customers but me. She was having a hard time with getting a screw loose on the handle bars. So after fueling I went over there and offered to help. She thanked me and said, if you weren't married I would marry you. I ignored the comment and went and payed for the gas.

My wife's son from a previous marriage, Eric, had moved in with us, coming up from Chicago to start a new beginning. He was using the same gas station as I was, and he knew that woman from the gas station also. She was there a lot. One day I came home from work, and Eric came up to me and was waiting for me to come home so he could tell me. He said "You're not going to believe this!" he said. "You know that woman at the gas station?" "Yeah! I said. He said, "I was getting my gas and went into the station to pay for it. There was a woman behind me waiting to pay for hers. This woman who was always there was at the cash register. So I paid for my gas and I left for home." He said, "When I got home, I parked and all of a sudden a car pulled up behind me and stopped. That woman who was behind me at the station got out and told me, "you know that lady at the gas station? Yes! Eric said. I used to go to school with her, that she is a he! He was a guy when he was at school.

Eric couldn't believe it, and neither could I. I had been ministering the word to her for a long time and didn't have a clue. This was clearly a move of God to send that woman over to our house, having no reason to come over and let me know because of how it turned out. We did not know this woman. She had no reason to follow Eric to the house to tell him this. God put it in her heart. Now I was faced with a decision. I didn't know how to handle that. I started going to another gas station for a while, but God dealt with me and said "what are you afraid of?" I said, nothing. So I started going back to that gas station again. There was nothing to be bothered about. So I went back and did business there and didn't say anything to him about knowing his condition, but I kept giving him the word of God. Then one day we were talking and he was making fun of angels, and I told him straight out "do not mock the things of God."! I left. Then the next time I was in there, I walked in and there was that woman who was now a man. I'm not kidding; she was a he again, dressed in guys clothes, with short hair.

He saw me and ran up to me happily saying "do you see a difference? I said yeah! When did you change back? He told me among other things that he was happy now and had a girlfriend who was great. He repented from being in sexual perversion, a transvestite. God had mercy on this guy. We don't know the circumstances of why people get to places like this, but God is merciful. God will deliver anyone willing to come to Him. I want you to note that it was the word of God doing the work, penetrating the heart and soul and bringing conviction to the sinner so they can see it for themselves and repent. We are dealing with a living God, not just words. His words are alive. Jesus did not condemn this guy but convicted him. He knew he neaded to repent. This is the love of God.

When I worked at the foundry, there were serious demon-possessed people there. I saw eyes roll back in their heads and tongues wagging like a demons. Meanness to fellow workers that would have been assault if it would have been done on the streets, and potential arrests. One of the guys at the foundry, let's call him Jackson. This guy had demons. I would talk to him at the coffee machine, hoping that the love of Christ would show through. I did not judge him and gave him respect, whereas nobody else would. Guys seemed to not want anything to do with him.

He had a darkness around him all the time. He liked to wear black clothes, but it was more than that; he looked evil.

In my junior high and early high school days, my friends and brothers would go to the local roller rink on Friday nights, mostly in the winter. This guy Jackson was there. His nickname was Cowboy. Everybody knew him with that name, and we all stayed away from him. He was known to be dangerous. In those days I was in my early teens. Cowboy was considerably older. He was around thirty when he was at the roller rink. He had that same darkness even in those days.

So it was really God that after all those years I get to talk to him in a new forum. Now I wasn't afraid of him and had Christ to boot.

So as we talked he told me some of his story. He was huge into drugs of all kinds, countless dealings with the law, shooting drugs behind his ears so there was no tracks on his arms for the police to find. He threw his girlfriend down the steps because he was mad at her for something. I could tell he had no emotion—he didn't feel anything. He was proud of it. Among other things he told me, he said that one day he told his ex-wife or girlfriend with whom they had a son together. He was coming over to get his son for visiting time. She said no! So he took two car ramps and went to her house, put the car ramps up against the house, backed up, hit the gas and drove through the wall and right into the kitchen of her house. Got out of the car, went, and grabbed the boy, got back in the car and left. He always seemed to slip through the fingers of the law. So this is what was in him.

So I kept on with him from time to time. Then he started getting sick and having health problems. He was put in the hospital, and I didn't see him at work for a while. God put it on my heart to go up and see him at the hospital. So I took time after work one day to go up and see him. I had no idea what I was going to say to him, so I prayed and just trusted God for the words.

So I get up to his room and knock on his door, and he said come on in. I walked in and said how are you doing? He was playing solitaire. He told me what the doctors were telling him. I still didn't know what to say. You have to be wise in these situations regarding how much to say. He never received the gospel, although I mentioned it to him before, a little here and a little there. He knew what I was, but in his case it wasn't really time for preaching as much as he needed unconditional love and mercy and not be rejected. He was used to being rejected. Jesus just wanted me to show him mercy. He was surprised to see me walk through the door. I am betting he never got any visitors outside of family members the whole time he was up there. As I was getting ready to leave after we talked a while, he said to me "this world would be a better place if people like you were in it." I said thank you. I believe my visit was a stepping stone to his future salvation. Some plant, some water, but God gives the increase (1 Cor. 3:6).

He came back to work finally and then all of a sudden he was gone again. He didn't show up for work anymore. Then the guys at work said, did you hear about Jackson? I said no. He has been arrested for pedophilia. "You're kidding I said." I got ahold of a newspaper and read where he was arrested for child molestation and pedophilia. Later he was given a prison sentence. God knew what he was doing and had mercy on him and wanted to see him repent. Yes, God will forgive all sexual perversity. All sin is sin. There is no greater sin or lesser sin. The greatest sin that anyone can commit that is not reversible is rejecting Jesus. As long as you are alive you have opportunity. But after death that door is closed forever.

Any sin can be erased by Jesus no matter how bad, but receiving him in your heart is the only way. Our sins are paid for either by Jesus, or you pay in eternity in the lake of fire, because sin has a price. You do not have access to Jesus's blood sacrifice for you unless you believe.

God has great joy in bringing you salvation. It is the goodness of God that leads us to repentance. He does not condemn. We are condemned already. He wants to give us a full pardon by making Him your savior and recieving Him. No matter how vile your sin, God will forgive it if you turn to Jesus. When God loves you uncon- ditionally, you can come to him with your most secret things, and He will not judge you but forgive you if you will repent. He is not wanting to condemn people but to have a relationship with you. This will cause you to love yourself also.

Did you know that heaven keeps books, a record of your daily activities and life? Nothing gets past God!! For those who refuse Christ, the books on you will be opened for judgment at the great white throne judgement. You will be judged according to your deeds, then the lambs book of life will be opened to see if your in it. When you are not found in the Book of life, you are then cast into the lake of fire forever. Your deeds will determan your degree of suffering. [Revelation 20:11,15.

So in reality, everyday you sin and dont have Christ, your sin debt is piling up.

God has written a book on your life, before you were created, of goal's and dreams and purpose He will accomplish in you. It is far better to follow Christ and follow the plan He wrote for your life at the beginning of time. You will love it. Delight yourselves also in the Lord and He will give you the desires of your heart [PSALM 37:4]

Romans 2:5,9 says,

But in accordance with your hardness and your unrepentant heart you are treasuring up for yourself wrath in the day of wrath and Revelation of the righteous judgment of God who will render to each one according to his deeds. Eternal life to those who by patient continuance in doing good seek for glory, honor and immortality; but to those who are self-seeking and do not obey the truth, but obey unrighteousness, indignation and wrath, tribulation and anguish on every soul that does evil.

Don't be deceived thinking God does not know your activities! Either Jesus's blood will pay for your sin or you will. Don't believe that just because you live a good long life without Christ that God approves or overlooks your sin. It will go against you to live that long and never come to the place of receiving Jesus.

For the believers who follows Christ, we are written in the book of life, according to Luke10:20 and Revelation20:15, and we are in the book of remembrance.

Malachi 3:16, 18 says,

Then those who feared the Lord spoke to one another, and the Lord listened and heard them; so a book of remembrance was written before Him for those who fear the Lord and meditate on His name. "They shall be mine says the Lord of hosts, on the day that I make them my jewels. I will spare them as a man spares his own son who serves him;

Then you shall again discern between the righteous and the wicked, between one who serves God and one who does not serve Him.

As I said before, we joined a local Word church. We were excited because we saw some of the gifts of the spirit, God's power move by the pastor and his wife. We never really saw that before. Through time we made a lot of friends and had great fellowship. We were on the praise team and involved in the church. There was an evangelist who came through out of Texas. His name was Donny. His wife was healed from breast cancer instantly by a miracle, and as a result he got saved and started evangelizing with a tent crusade across America. Our praise team got to do the music for the tent crusade for weeks. It was great and a lot of fun. We went to some meetings in Green Lake, Wisconsin, where we saw some great preachers and Kenneth Hagen. I was growing in the word. Our church got a different pastor over time and asked me if I wanted to be an elder. I said yes. So as I was doing that I was getting a real burden from the Lord for guys. They were hurting in a lot of ways that they would not show the world.

I was from the same background. As I became friends with some of them and as their guards went down, I started to see their pain. Guys keep a lot of things in; when we hurt, we usually don't tell anybody because we don't want to appear weak, but also we don't know who to trust and who would care. The love of God pulls these things out. I heard a lot of teaching on how husbands were supposed to love their wives but very little on men and their needs. We were encouraged in the Lord.

I really had compassion on roughnecks because I was one. A lot of the workers at the foundry were acquainted with prison including my foreman and boss, Mike.

After I was saved, God led me to visit these people, and one of them was my old boss. He quit the foundry and started his own business in buying scrap metal and selling it. God had me stop at his house and give him the gospel. I am happy to say that he sat down and listened to me; he knew what I was.

So the pastor let me sponsor a maximize manhood series at the church. It was a taped series we ran through ten weeks. It was good, and we had a good turnout. We prayed, talked, and confessed. We had one guy who was strapped to his bed and beaten as a boy by his mother, and other things. The thing that caught my attention is, you can have guys that are in suits that look good on the outside but are all torn up on the inside and need deliverance. So many walk around acting like they don't have a care in the world, but they are all torn up inside. Jesus can deliver you of all your pain, men, if you will humble yourself, receive him, and trust the promises. Don't stay the way you are. Don't give Satan one more day of beating you over the head with your past. Jesus will deliver you of anything you will be honest about and bring to the surface to Him and confess. He loves you.

He has perfect courage, perfect strength, perfect love. He is the perfect man. showing us how God ordained men to be.

I have heard it said that if Satan got your past, don't give him your future. Jesus can heal every secret pain and sin you have if you will verbally give it to Him and lay it at his feet. He is the perfect man. He makes us completed. God wants us happy and contented in Him. Past guilt and pain steals it.

Through a prophecy God gave us, we went on vacation in 1991 out to Montana to visit friends. As we were going through the Badlands of South Dakota, we stopped off at a site where the movie *Dancing with Wolves* was made. We were able to see some of the props of the movie. We got to pet the horse, Cisco from the movie. Then we went to a sight seeing pull off, and we got out of the van and were looking at the Badlands. As we were there, another couple was there standing away from us. As we were looking at the incredible view. I noticed that the other couple's car was smoking from under the hood a little. So I went up to him and brought it to his attention. He said oh yeah. So we looked under the hood and it was no big deal; it was a little oil on the manifold.

So we started talking. He asked me what's your name and where I was from and I said I'm Marty from Appleton Wisconsin. I asked him, what's your name? He said "John Hughes." "Where are you from? I asked? He said Hollywood. He said that they were heading back there right now, coming from Chicago. I asked, what do you do there? He said I am a movie producer actually. I said really! What movies have you produced? He said his recent one was *Home Alone*. I had heard of it but never saw it. He also made *Ferris Bueller's Day Off* and *Vacation*. So I started talking to him about California and the fires even back then and drought. I said there is a lot of wickedness there and that the constant disasters are happening to California because God is shaking California to get their attention to repent. I got the impression that hollywood morality bothered him as we talked. I talked to him about Jesus.

John Hughes talked to me about that subject. I talked to him about Jesus and salvation. Then he got going. I knew that this was an appointment from God for him, to give him an opportunity to get saved. He would have been very hard to get to talk to in his world. Later I went to a library and got a book on John Hughes's movie carrier, with a commentary on the inside cover to be sure that he was telling me the truth because I did not know who he was.

The picture on the inside cover was the guy I talked to. God had led us to go out to Montana at that time, and we did not know what God had in store for us. This was clearly an appointment God gave us to meet John, and as we went on our trip other things happened also.

This was in 1991. John died in 2009, but it was a great opportunity to be able to talk to someone like that about their salvation. Actors, producers, political leaders, or a gas station attendant. Makes no difference. God is no respector of persons. He will save anybody willing.

In the mid-1990s I received a letter without any return address. It was not traceable. In it, the letter said, "This is a onetime offer and will never be offered to me again! It said things like, "if you want to be rich, and famous and have multitudes love you, I am to call this particular number on the letter within in something like 48 hours. I no longer have the letter. If I don't call by then the offer is withdrawn. I will never be offered this again. The letter also gave the names of famous people and entertainers who took this offer as examples, and I could have it too. I did not take this offer! I knew it was to sell my soul so I could have the world's goods, but sell my soul in the process. I knew it was from the new world order. This would have taken me out of my life with Jesus and my ministry and sentenced me to hell.

It was amazing really because they found me in a little hick town in Missouri. It was the ultimate temptation for me. Satan offered the world to Jesus in the desert.

In [Matthew 4:8,10] And again the devil took Him up to an exceedingly high mountain, and showed Him all the kingdoms of the world and their glory. And he said to him, "all these things I will give you if you will fall down and worship me" then Jesus said to him, "away with you Satan, for it is written! You shall worship the Lord your God and him only you shall serve." Then Satan left Him.

This temptation was designed for Jesus to break away from the will of His Father. It would have destroyed his ability to be Savior and would have rendered him powerless. As long as Jesus stayed in unity with the Father, Satan couldn't touch him. That letter to me would have destroyed my life and broken me away from the Father and rendered me powerless.

God is calling us to repentance and salvation, Hollywood actors and executives, and producers, and business people. The mover and shakers of the world system, as well as the common population. Become uncommon by receiving Jesus Christ and becoming the son or daughter of the king. I guarantee you that God will forgive you of all things wicked you ever did and wipe the slate clean. He loves you and loves to do that. The gospel of Christ is to the whole world. No one is left out. Even if you sold your soul to Satan but want out and are willing to come to Him for real wanting out, you can be saved.

Forget what you have heard in religion. Start over by the real thing. Receive Jesus, repent, and you are on your way without a religion.

When I started getting dreams from God in the late 1980s they started out on a small scale first like things in my life, including relationships. God would tell me things ahead of time with them, and then I would see them happen. Then He would start telling me things in dreams about work situations and people I was ministering to. I would get a dream concerning it and then see it happen. Warning dreams about coming attacks through people at work and then I would see them happen, so I was getting confident about getting dreams from God and that they were really from Him. They are always very vivid, like on a flat screen tv. They have a starting point and an ending point.

Later after the year 2000 came, I was getting audible visits from the Lord at my house. God was dealing with me about getting up in the morning early and get into fellowship and the word with Him before I went to work. He woke me up one morning at 4:30 a.m. and as I was up, He put it in my heart to get in the word with Him. I got lazy and looked at the clock and lay back down, happy I had a little more time to sleep. As soon as I laid down and didn't obey, there was a sudden audible explosion of thunder that cracked about five inches above my head. I heard it with my ears! Loud!

I had made God furious. It was like him stomping in anger. He kept dealing with me on this. Audible alarm clocks would go off in my room from time to time that were not there. Different sounds every time. These were audible sounds I was hearing loud and clear. And it was not my own alarm clock. That was always set for later to go on. The sounds were sometimes like a laser like massive power. Other times it was an audible knock like at a door right next to my head where there was no wood. Always at the same time in the morning. God wanting the first part of my day with Him. God wanted the first part of my day with Him. One day a bolt of lightning struck my back yard 40 feet from my bedroom window where I was looking out of right in front of me just as I was waking up. WOW!

One time as I was sleeping, I was sleeping late from working a second job at the TV station, twelve-hour shifts as master control operator, running the programming. So as I was sleeping on my side I heard a voice behind me say, "Are you still sleeping?" It was Jesus in my room. I turned around, but he was already gone. I got the message finally and repented, and now I get in the word at any time of the day also. This was a serious matter to Jesus.

I worked the night shift at the TV station for three-and-one-half years. As time went on I started seeing apparitions, ghost like human forms walking through the halls by the newsroom and in the control room where I was. I was the only one there at night, and sometimes I would see as many as three in one night. It occurred to me that these demons were there to influence the news. We had live news, weather, sports studio.

Generally the news is bad news, which then makes people depressed and cynical and distrusting of others. Satan loves the bad news and the gossip of news because it steals people's faith and takes their hope and promotes fear! Devils feed on fear. News produces unbelief. Making the worlds problems so big that people believe their is no hope and the problems are bigger than God. What you concentrate on you become like. The bible is posative and full of hope.

I talked to the daytime master control operator when he came in on his shift, and I told him that it was busy here last night. He said, "what do you mean? I said I saw apparitions, ghosts, walking around the halls last night. He said, "oh we see them all the time and we make jokes about it. Good news builds hope; bad news tries to kill hope.

God started giving me dreams on a larger scale also visions.

Joel 2:28 says, "It shall come to pass afterward that I will pour out my spirit on all flesh; your sons and your daughters shall prophesy, your old men shall dream dreams, your young men shall see visions. That time is right now.

I had a dream about America in 1994.

I saw all the stars of heaven as I was looking up into the sky. Then suddenly one set of stars formed together and formed the shape of a eagle. Its wings were in the down position like the back of a quarter. It was just the outline like when you trace something on paper, only it was made up with stars. Huge. Then suddenly another set of stars formed next to the eagle in the shape of a grizzly bear. Massive. all made of stars. The bear grabbed the eagle by the throat, and as he did, the eagle turned into the shape of a vulture. Instantly. So the bear didn't kill an eagle but a vulture. America became an unclean and a filthy bird in the eyes of God. The bear killed the vulture. End of dream. Read the book of [Revelation chapter 18:2].

God is giving America a chance to repent and turn to Him before the rest of America will have to be judged by Him because of rebellion, and her sin's have reached to heaven, and God has remembered her iniquities. [REVELATION 18:5] There are those who willl never turn to Christ.

At the time of the release of this book God is taking the wicked leaders out of government and hollywood and churches where pastors are preaching a compromised message. God put Donald trump in office to get rid of the swamp so we would not have to live in fear of retribution for standind up for our faith in Christ. We now have another window of oppertunity to recieve Jesus as Lord before the final blow to America. How long it will last, I dont know. Dont waste time.

America belongs to God. It was founded by a people who loved God and wanted a place of freedom where they could worship God without fear of attack, torture, or any retribution. God decides when America falls. Meanwhile, take this time to get right with God so you don't fall with it. Sin is what will ultimately destroy America. Sin must be judged.

God warns because he loves the people. The judgments of the book of Revelation will happen because it is written. God knows his timing.

I believe America is Babylon the great that has fallen in chapter 18 of the book of revelation.

[Revelation 18:13] Among the merchadise destroyed in Babylon will be; "cinnamon and incence, fragrant oil and frankincence, wine, oil, fine flour and wheat, cattle and sheep, horses and chariots, and bodies and souls of men.

So human trafficing we see today is buying bodys and souls of men. how close are we?

After these things I saw another angel coming down from heaven, having great authority, and the earth was illuminated with his glory. And he cried mightily with a loud voice, saying, Babylon the great has fallen, is fallen, and has become a habitation of demons, a prison for every foul spirit, and a cage for every unclean and hated bird. (Rev. 18: 1–2) America.

Read the whole chapter; this is what I saw in the dream, the unclean bird. The vulture that was killed.

I had another dream November 14, 2005. Note the time of this dream.

I was standing in the air about forty feet above a highway, As a watchman. I was in Ohio above I-80 looking east. And a car full of young people, like college age and high school age people were drinking and partying in an open-top vehicle, like a sun roof or open-top jeep. They were going down the highway, booze bottles in their hands, without a care in the world. They were screaming and partying. I was watching them.

The sky was a dark gray purple color, dangerous as far as I could see. All over the north. Massive storm! And all of a sudden, a pair of wings formed in the sky to the north, and then a porcelain-like human figure formed between them. Bright White. It was a huge angel! About the size of a city. Then the angel started to move across the sky. It was heading across the path of the partying kids. The angel started forming into a horse and changing colors as it moved through the sky. First was a white horse. Then a red horse. And then a black horse. The last horse color was the pale horse of death. These were the four horses of the apocalypse. [Revelation 6:1,8]

The horses were intersecting with the carload of people. The last one being death. I yelled to the people in the car. Don't you see what you are heading into? Death! Stop!!, don't you see this coming? I even pointed to it. They didn't see it and refused to look. Instead they looked back at me with hateful, murderous eyes to tell me to shut up. They would have killed me if they could have. They looked at me as if to say, don't tell us anything. They wanted to kill me!! God's judgment was heading right for them

95

because of their ignoring His word, even when God tried to warn them. They refused to repent and return to God. They ignored all warnings. They only looked at me and refused to look at the impending judgment.

The scripture for this dream is in these two scriptures: [Revelation 6], and also [Jeremiah 6:16, 20].

This dream is for today! Repent before you are too far gone with a hard heart, and you are caught like a bird in a snare. Stop idoling your own way. Turn to Jesus whom God has sent to you that you will not have to suffer judgment.

The rider on the white horse I believe is religion. Looking righteous, preaching false doctrine in order to lead people astray, causing them to fall short of salvation and repentance. These four horses are seals being released by the lamb; Jesus. Judgment breaks mens pride if you survive it and it will bring you to the place of taking God into your life.

Pharaoh of Egypt refused to listen to Moses message straight from God to him, so judgment had to precede Moses message. drought, plagues, blood in the river, food supply ate by locusts and finally their first born children being killed by the angel of death, to get pharaohs heart to change and let the people go. These plagues were sent against the false gods of Egypt. God showing Himself greater than any false god of this earth. Unfortunately, many in America and the world will have to go through this because they would not earlier recieve the love of Gods message of salvation because of the pride and stubborness of their own hearts.

[Romans 2:5] But in accordance with your hardness and your impenitent heart you are treasuring up for yourself wrath in the day of wrath and revelation of the righteous judgment of God.

2nd Timothy 3:12,13

Yes, and all who desire to live godly in Christ will suffer persecution. But evil men and imposters will grow worse and worse, deceiving and being deceived.

We must realize that just because we sin without Jesus daily and nothing happens to us, it is all piling up and recorded in heaven. There will be a day of wrath for those who refuse to turn to Jesus and stop sinning against God. God keeps records on personal sin and a nations sin as a whole. He longs to erase it through repentance.

This has been my experience for years. So few people want to hear the word and be saved. They would rather hold on to their selfish world of me and live by the beliefs they have developed and chosen and keep Jesus out, than avoid death and judgment by receiving Jesus.

Note, in my dream, the people in the jeep didn't say anything to me because they had no excuse, there wouldn't have been anything they could have said to justify their ignoring the warning. There is time to repent and turn to Christ yet before it's too late. God has a life and a hope for the young people who party and those who do not. I was one of them once. An alcoholic! That lifestyle is empty and will disappoint you and leave you empty inside. God is calling you to something better and higher. Remember that Satan not only lies to those who oppose him but also lies to those who work with him and for him and do his bidding. He will ultimately kill his followers.

Don't be deceived into thinking that if you remain ignorant of God and his word that you get a free pass to heaven. Not true. God Himself knows how many opportunities you have had and refused. It is all recorded in the books kept on every person in heaven (Rev. 20:11, 15). If you choose to remain ignorant, you have already made your choice.

God gave me another dream on May 8, 2014, about America.

This was during the Obama Presidency. I believe I was being used for intersession, and this event was fixing to take place before God intervened by replacing Obama and hearing the prayers of His saints in America who Know Him. God loves this nation. But He is looking for a nation of people He can call His own.

It is a very serious thing who gets into the White house because the president covers the nation and can let in evil spirits or Gods will into the nation to bless it or curse it. If the nation decides to put a wicked president in by votes, then the nation will suffer the consequences of it also. Put a righteous man in and the nation will start to benefit.

May 8th, 2014

[I had two dreams.] The same dream two nights in a row. A repeat. I was standing about twenty feet off the ground. I was about in the Georgia area looking east and watching a ravaging army coming from the east and heading west. They were killing without mercy, man, woman, and child, chasing them. They were marching on US shores from the east moving west. At first I thought they were the Nazis, but I quickly realized they were far worse. I did not see markings on their uniforms. I saw a wooden pallet or a block-like object, that people were tripping on as they were chased out. Then I saw a book appear in my hand. On one side it said army from hell. Then it turned over by itself and it said army from hell. This happened the same exact way the next night. God confirming it.

Note the pallet like or block-like object that the people were tripping on tells me that this army is going to be a stumbling block for many because they were not ready in Christ! This lines up with the bible in the book of Jeremiah 6:21-30: "Behold I lay a stumbling block for this people. cont.. [Jeremiah chapter 51.]

[1 Peter 2: 7,8] Therefore to you who believe, He is precious; but to those who are disobedient, the stone which the builders rejected has become the chief corner stone; and a stone of stumbling and rock of offense" They stumble being disobedient to the word, which they also were appointed.

The stumbling block the people were tripping on as they were running away was their own idolatry! Sin is a stumbling block. The things in their lives they put before the Lord instead of Jesus being first that kept them from being prepared for such a time as this that they were going through. Here is the scripture for that.

[Isaiah 57:11–13] "And of whom have you been afraid or feared, that you have lied and not remembered me, nor taken it to heart? Is it not because I have held my peace from of old and you do not fear me? I will declare your righteousness and your works, and they will not profit you. When you cry out, let your collection of idols deliver you. But the wind will carry them all away, a breath will take them. But he who puts his trust in Me shall possess the land, and shall inherit My holy mountain."

These dreams are warnings so you can get prepared while there is time. God warns because it is all an act of your own will.

His salvation is ready. When will you be?!!!

I believe that this army will come one day when America falls, but in Gods time. not satans and mans time. God is still bringing in souls daily. as I have studied the bible for years I have seen from the Lord that He doesnt judge a nation until the sin has become so grievous that it has to be judged. God gives much warning first. Babylon the Great, aka, America,s sin has reached up to heaven before Gods judgment finally falls. [Revelation 18:5].

I do not know the time of this army invasion. Warnings are good to save lives. We warn for tornadoes, hurricanes, snow fall, and so on to save lives. Repent while there is time. This nation needs to seriously repent so as to put off judgment as long as possible.

I had a dream on May 1, 2015, of a city in America. It looked like New York. I felt it was New York; anyway, it had the appearance of it. As I was sleeping I was in a three-dimensional world, like I was physically there. I found myself in a crashed van turned on its side. I was in the back of the van. I was awake in the dream and regained consciousness. I looked at my situation and thought I got knocked out in a car accident, but I didn't remember any accident. So I started crawling out of the van, checking my body. This was so real that my arms were moving for real physically in the chair I was sleeping in. It was that real. I had no bodily damage or pain at all. So I got outside of the van and saw no human life anywhere yet. The city was bombed out. I saw a sky scraper with the top totally missing. There was debris everywhere, but not real bad. Across the street there was a limousine sitting on its chassis, all wheels gone, and it looked like it had been on fire. The luxury of America gone.

I was reminded of Revelation 18:14. As I was looking at the damage, a tow truck pulled up and hooked up to the van I was in and the person was going to take it away, I tried to stop that person because the van I thought was mine but quickly realized that everything was junk. This tow truck driver a survivor was trying to get back the old life by picking this van up, but it was useless. Everything was destroyed. I don't know the timing of this event.

I have told you my dreams that I believe through experience God gave me. I have had a track record of seeing dreams come to pass. I do not know when these things will happen. I'm not setting dates of any kind. Mystery Babylon-America will be destroyed one day because of her sin. It has reached to heaven, and God has remembered her. [Revelation 18:5] Keep your eyes on your relationship with the Lord Jesus. Keep yourself ready. Don't fear at all; ask Christ in, and He will keep you. Rest in Christ and realize He has all things under His control. Warnings are given early because God loves people and gives them time to get prepared and not to set your hearts on the things of the earth. God takes care of His own. If the nation repents and turns to God and His Son Jesus it can stop events or delay them. God will protect those who are His. He will sustain his own.

The ones who should fear are the people who don't want Christ as their Lord and Savior.

Scripture for this is Luke 19:27: But bring here those enemies of mine, who did not want me to reign over them, and slay them before me."

2nd Chronicles 7:14: "If my people who are called by my name will humble themselves, and pray and seek my face, and turn from their wicked ways, then I will hear from heaven and will forgive their sin and heal their land.

I had another dream October 18, 2008; note the date of the dream:

This was about President-elect Obama:

I was standing under some kind of platform, a stage, at some kind of stadium. I could hear crowds cheering above me like a large football stadium. I was under the platform so I did not know exactly where I was. I saw Obama laying on a table about ten feet from me. He was totally motionless and still. He looked lifeless. He was strapped down with about five straps. [total bondage] Then the table started lifting up on a hydraulic system, lifting Obama higher and higher. Then a hatch opened up on the stage floor, and he was lifted up through it. But as he was coming to the top, the straps let go by themselves, and then life started coming into his body, and as he went through the hole in the floor, he lifted his hands up above his head like he was some great person, and that's when the crowd saw him and screams and cheers went out all over the stadium. But none of them saw what I saw. Some kind of life went into him. I knew it was bad. Evil. Obama was activated with something new. At the stadium, end of dream. He was being worshiped.

I knew next to nothing about Obama. But later I realized after seeing a news clip on television, that what I was seeing and where I was standing in the dream was in Mile High Stadium in Colorado on his acceptance speech for the Democratic nomination. I did not know it until I saw it on tv. I instantly knew, that's where I was in the dream. He did not come through a door in the floor, but God was showing me what was going on in the spiritual realm with him. The affect he wanted to have on the people.

I then found out later that Obama visited a museum in Germany with the altar of Zeus. A Greek God of the lightning, the sky, and thunder, in ancient Greek mythology. Just before his nomination in Mile High Stadium.

Obama had the Greek altar of Zeus then replicated at Mile High Stadium for his acceptance speech. Trying to bring in the worship of a man. A false god.

Adam and Eve ate from the tree of the knowledge of good and evil. That is what we are seeing right now in life, the knowledge of good and evil is in the earth right now!! We are all aware that there is good and evil. We are all aware of making good choices or bad choices. You must choose whom you will serve. You have free will to choose. Evil will be judged and eliminated by God. If you choose good, you must choose Jesus.

Earth is a taste of heaven and hell. If you refuse Christ or haven't accepted him yet, demons have access to your life, and they are torturers! Sickness, disease, evil thoughts, tormenting fear, temptations of hate, lust, unforgiveness addictions, etc.—these are small portions of torture from the satanic realm!

[Second Corinthians 4:4] calls Satan the God of this world. So we have Satan and God both battling for the souls of men both on the earth at this time. God is going to destroy Satan in the lake of fire, and Christ will rule the earth as a single ruler along with us the saved church. We believers will be ruling with Him. Satan and All demons will be thrown in the lake of fire along with the people who followed him.

Our taste of heaven is the good things that we have in the earth. Skills, talents, jobs, health, rain, beauty of the earth, family, developed skills, your house. Creativity. Pleasures and hobbies that we do. We have both good and evil on the earth. We must make the choice if we want good to grow and continue all the way to heaven where there are pleasures for ever more (Ps. 16:11).

Romans 2:7 states, Eternal life to those who by patient continuance in doing good seek for glory, honor, and immortality.

Continuing with my testimony. I was having appendicitis attacks at work and at different times. I believe all sickness and disease is from Satan. I was rebuking it and binding the devil, so that it would go away. This went on for some time. Then one day it was really bad. My son John and I were going down the road in my van and a real bad attack came that made me double over. It was hard to drive. I knew I had to do one of two things: either go straight to the hospital or go home and get in the Bible right away and believe God. It was bad. So I went home, and my wife was going to the store, so she took the kids and left.

So I went into my bedroom and knelt on the floor next to the bed, opened my Bible to the healing scriptures. I went to 1st Peter 2:24, which says, "Who Himself bore our sins in his own body on the tree, that we having died to sins might live for righteousness- by whose stripes we are healed."

Then I went to [ISAIAH 53:4,5] "Surely He has born our griefs and carried our sorrows; we esteemed him stricken, smitten by God and afflicted. He was wounded for our transgressions, he was bruised for our iniquities; the chastisement of our peace was upon him, and by his stripes we are healed."

I was praying for about forty-five minutes quoting these scriptures and rebuking the devil in the name of Jesus, and all of a sudden it was gone. Totally gone, like it was just shut off. Praise God, I was excited. The demonic infirmity had to leave. I went back to putting a new countertop in my kitchen just minutes after I was healed. Only God and his word can do this.

We moved to Missouri to help a ministry. When we got there I had no idea where I was going to work. There was a new business in the area called Premium Standard Farms. So I went there and applied. Within two weeks I got a job there. This is a hog husbandry place with its own kill plant. A large investment in the area. They breed and raise their own hogs to market weight, then send them to the kill plant for processing. From birth to the box, all one company.

I worked in a sow unit, from breeding to ween pigs. I stayed there for about three months. It was uninteresting for me because I was from the city, it was new for me, and the pay was low. But God opened a new door for me. They had a maintenance department. So I was able to transfer to that department through an internal transfer. Praise God. I did good and eventually I got a company truck. God was blessing me in it. Eventually I was given my own grow finish farm to take care of. I loved doing it and figuring out electrical problems and building repairs plus plumbing and water pumps. It was great. Eventually I was asked to be the superintendent over half of their grow finish units and their personnel. God was blessing me.

I was getting a lot of dreams from God, warnings of people in my life. He was giving me warnings about my own family members, because I was trying to get them saved. We had not seen each other in years because they didn't want anything to do with me as long as I was talking about Christ.

In about 1987

God gave me a dream about my brother , that he was not receiving the message. I saw him in his house commanding an electronic device that would lock the doors and turn lights on just by voice command. This was in about 1987. I was seeing the Siri device in his house and that he was at this time in the world system. He wasnt ready yet to receive Christ. I had been praying for him.

God gave me a dream about my parents when I was in Missouri because I was thinking about going and visiting my family in Wisconsin. At this point I hadn't seen them for about ten years.

[Dream] I saw myself sitting in my pickup truck with the front of the truck pointed towards Wisconsin, but the truck was stationary, not moving. My mom and dad were standing in the front of the truck, with two notebooks on the hood of my truck, one in front of each of them. In the notebooks they were writing down everything they could find wrong with me, keeping a record to justify themselves of why they weren't receiving Christ.

By writing down all my flaws that they knew, they would just give me a fight if I went down there. Justifying themselves to not accept the gospel. Some years later I told my dad that dream because he was asking why I didn't come down to visit and I told him that dream God gave me about him and ma. He said, "So what if we were?" He admitted it. So God was warning me of what I was walking into. So I didn't go up to visit then. I was learning to let God fight my battles with people who hated me or persecuted me.

This is a typical tactic of people. to point at the messenger and accuse me so that they dont have to listen; Justifying themselves in their own mind when they dont understand that I had already went to Jesus with my sin, gave my life to Christ and had my sins forgiven under His blood. I was not the same person they thought I was. Jesus told me to preach.

Once I was known to be a Christian a lot of people copped an attitude towards me. But I was also learning how to deal with people the Jesus way by forgiving, and showing kindness when they did not. It was hard, and I had a lot of problem with my own flesh and old attitudes of hitting them, habits I still had to address. When I was faced with trouble from someone else or they did something I didn't like, I would find out what was still in me that had to be repented of and put under the blood of Jesus. Troubles have a way of showing you that, bringing out the worst or the best.

The longer I walked with the Lord the less people bothered me because I was giving my battles to Christ. I was getting more peace. I was still struggling with authority figures such as bosses because I saw so much abuse of authority in my house growing, up and it caused a distrust of authority in general. But the problem was mine; bosses have to be bosses. I went through some really painful corrections to learn that lesson and to get the rebellion out of me and follow protocol. I had been to many human resources meetings where I was called in and they would try to write me up for something or fire me. But I always walked out. I saw two different bosses from two different companies sit across from me in human resources and just become uninterested and walk out.

My pastors were a big help in that. I was a maintenance superintendent and very independent. I liked working alone and didn't like asking for help unless it was unavoidable. This came back to bite me later on. I volunteered to work a weekend that eight recycle pumps had to be restarted that were previously acid treated. They had to run or the sulfuric acid would destroy the seals. So I had one day to do it. To make a long story short, I was having a hard time with some of them but kept going to the next one. So I got about five or six going but I couldn't get two or three, so the day was getting dark, so I decided to come back the next day. I did not call anyone for help to speed the process. Then the next day, Monday, the pump crew went down to the pumps ahead of me and got their before me. They opened up one of the pumps and got a little sulfuric acid on his boots. That was a safety hazard that I was responsible for. As a result I lost my job.

Later I was hired at the kill plant and got a good job as a groundskeeper God was doing it. It was an excellent job. My pastors and I were praying I get a good job. God answered it. I did this job for years; there was a lot of on the job training. Snow removal, grass cutting, forklift, bobcat work, moving outside materials where ever they needed to go, and many trips taken for the plant to get parts or deliver parts. It was a job I really liked. I went through two different bosses over the time, and my third boss was my challenge from Satan.

This particular boss didn't like me from the start—he even said it. This particular guy was in charge of the environmental things that happened at the plant, anything that escaped the property, such as spills of any kind. Ground water contamination, anything escaping into the air and what comes onto the property that could potentially spill or contaminate. So he was in charge of land and water, answering to the DNR and EPA. Also he was in charge of waste water and fresh water. This guy was now my boss. I was told that he used to say that if he ever got the groundskeeper job under him he would get rid of me.

So this is what I was up against. I worked for him for some years, and he was always trying to trip me up. Asking testing questions and making sure that when I screwed up he would really get the most out of it. It was so bad, I knew it was a demon in him, aggravating me. He was what the world would call a narcissist. I could feel that he was just lying in wait for me to make the wrong move so he could fire me. This was spiritual warfare. My pastor's wife would call me up and tell me that Satan's trying to get your job. At first I didn't want to believe it, but it was getting obvious. He made my life a small living hell, trying to entrap me any time he could but really didn't have anything that would get me fired because I was doing my job.

Foot note; When I say satan is trying to get my job, or satan is attacking me, I am not calling people satan. But demons are influencing these people against me and they are not aware of it.

Then it happened. One day I was mowing around the water plant where his office is, and I accidently touched the cement with the lawn mower blade and it made a buzzing noise. I backed off, and it stopped. His door was open, and he heard it; his boss was with him out of Kansas City, and that's all it took. God told me, he is going to come out to attack my job. So his boss left, and sure enough he came out and approached me and said when your job affects my job, then it's time for you to leave. His boss heard the lawn mower and asked about it. That's all it took. So he said to me, "we can go to human resources right now, and we will walk you out, or I will give you a month to find another job. I said I will find another job. He said okay. He thought he really had me this time.

So I went home that night and God gave me a dream concerning this situation:

[Dream] I saw the water plant where my boss's office was. I was standing in front of the building. Then I looked to my left, and there stood Jesus. He had a white robe with a gold sash, but he did not let me see his face. There was a small crocodile crawling up his leg and snapping at him. He said to me, "Do what I do," and he took the crocodile attacking him, grabbed it, and threw it into the air, and it came back down and hit the ground and died. There was the exact same size crocodile crawling up my leg attacking me and snapping. So I grabbed the one attacking me. It hurt, but not much, and I threw it into the air like Jesus did, and it came back down and hit the ground and died.

Then Jesus disappeared. End of dream.

This evil spirit that was attacking me through my boss was really attacking Jesus in me, so it was the Lord's battle.

Later I realized that the reason it was a crocodile was that it was a figure of my boss, the spirit working in him, because he is in charge of land and water on the plant property, and a crocodile is a land and water amphibian. A serpent. That also represents a heartless serpent that is Satan, the spirit that was operating in my boss. The crocodile was a perfect fit.

So I woke up but didn't know what was going to happen next. God showed me that the battle was His, and it was really Jesus in me being attacked. Satan hates the spirit of God. So he hates the children of God. Jesus gave me the victory—but how? My answer came shortly in a few days.

The corporate people came from Kansas City to the plant and gave the employees a survey to fill out. We didn't put our names on it. The questions were about our particular department that we worked in. They were a performance sheet on our bosses. A lot of questions about different categories, like how well do they communicate, do they make sure you know your job, what are dislikes and likes, etc. Our names didn't go on to protect the employee from retribution from supervisors. So there I was with this sheet.

Do I tell everything that has been going on or should I just play it down? I decided to tell all in detail. Nobody knew what was going on but me and him, and he already told me to look for another job. So I had nothing to lose. So being honest and not making more of something than it really was, I told it all. I wrote intimidation, entrapment, threats, never knowing if I am going to keep my job to the next day, etc. A lot of questions were scaled from 1 to 10 questions. At the bottom was an area for freelance comments. I spilled everything that I could think of. Then I turned my paper in.

We are a small group of people in my department, so even without names on the sheet, I knew he would be able to figure out from my sheet who I was.

The sheets went to the corporate bosses for evaluation and then in turn they would talk to the supervisors. It was an intervention from Jesus, perfect timing with the dream.

About a week later, my boss was hauled into a meeting and questioned about the sheet. He was shocked at the things on the sheet. All the supervisors lost their yearly bonuses that year, a huge chunk of money! Then all of a sudden my boss was like a different person, I'm not kidding! He was courteous, helpful, went out of his way to make sure everything was okay, made sure I understood what he needed done, and on and on.

It was remarkable. He wasn't doing it because he had to; that demon that Jesus broke off of him is what did it. He was totally different. We kidded around over the years and sometimes we just sat and talked. This went on for years. Praise God how He watches over His people. I kept my job for years.!!

Then there was another incident. Because there was only one grounds keeper, me! There were people who wanted that job too so they could be outside.

I had repeated dreams that someone was trying to steal my job. In the dream I saw the front of the plant and someone trying to steal my job. I had no idea who and there was no evidence of it. Then my pastor's wife called me one day and said that God told her that someone was trying to steal my job. This was a week after I already had the dream. God already warned me about it. So God gave me two confirmations. I came to work one day and saw some of the bushes trimmed that I didn't do. Then the guy who did it came up to me and told me, he asked the head of human resources if he could have some overtime working outside after work. He said that he used to work for a landscaping company in Kansas City.

He was trying to come in through the back door, telling HR he could do a better job. There was nothing I could do about it if human resources gave him the okay to work outside, but Jesus took care of it again. That guy suddenly disappeared. He got hurt at home somehow. After some time he came back to work, and I had to take gas out to him with the company truck because he couldn't get all the way to work. I saw God give me the total victory over this guy being used by Satan. Shortly afterward he was escorted off the property, fired! He was escorted away by three supervisors. Praise God again.

Time would fail me to write everything that God has done for me over all the years so far and the revelations, but here are some highlights that mean a lot to me. There were so many enemies that hated me for no reason, and I stood up to them. I don't choose to fear man. Some are dead, others God got out of the way and fired.

I fell eleven feet off a ladder one time, and when I hit the ground I got up slow to be sure that I didn't break anything. I was okay except that I broke one finger. I thought that was pretty good considering what could have happened. I grabbed my finger with my other hand and started rebuking unbelief and started quoting the healing scriptures over it and thanking Jesus for my healing. The finger was healed in about fifteen minutes. Praise the Lord!!!!!

Another time I was at work, pulling gams of steel across a monorail, each weighing about five pounds. One fell off and hit me in the nose and broke it. I was bleeding like a stuck hog. I ran down to the nurses office. They worked on me for more than an hour to stop the bleeding and were debating about taking me to the hospital. But over time they were able to slow the bleeding down. I walked around on light duty the rest of the day. If I bent over, it would start bleeding again. This went on into the weekend. At church the pastor called me forward to pray for my nose. They prayed and I didn't feel any different, but it wasn't over yet. That Sunday night I was sitting on the couch reading my Bible and suddenly I felt an invisible finger swipe across the right side of my nose, then I felt a finger swipe across the left side. I saw no fingers, but I felt them. I checked my nose, and it was completely healed. Praise God again!!!! I never bleed again.

A pastor friend of mine who is now deceased told me what happened to him as we were trading stories. In Wisconsin in the sixties and seventies it was a common practice to put cardboard in front of your car radiator to get the engine hotter in the winter. He went to remove his one day out of a van and got three fingers cut off of his hand because he got his hand to close to the fan blades. They were just hanging there by the skin. He wrapped his hand with a rag and started rebuking fear and started quoting the healing scriptures over his hand as he ran into the bathroom of the church, thanking Jesus for his healing. As he took the rag off, his fingers were completely reattached. No scar either. These are the benefits of being a child of God if you can believe.

God is still dealing with me to get up in the morning. On April 22, 2014, at 4:55 a.m., God woke me up again. I have an alarm clock that makes a certain sound, and when it sounds off, it stays beeping until I turn it off. I was sleeping, and I suddenly heard a loud buzzing sound, like the sound of electrical power, like a large bolt of electricity. Audibly. It was right in the middle of the room, away from any wall or shelf or clock. Midair. Always in the same time of the morning, waking me up.

On July 7, 2013, at 4:45 a.m. I was asleep and all of a sudden a loud laser shot off in the middle of the room. It was an electrical sound, like power. My alarm clock didn't go off yet. The sound was from the middle of the room. It was audible. He was still working on me to get me up in the morning.

One time I had some sinful thoughts in my mind. Then all of a sudden right behind me was this audible sound of metal clanking like shackles and chains on a prisoner, and it was heading towards my back door out of the house. I got the message and quickly repented. I don't want the bonds of sin on me. The shackles were being removed. I heard them leave.

In spring of 2016; I was watching a NASA documentary about the Apollo space program. Suddenly I heard an audible trumpet blast in my living room about 4 feet from me. I knew the Lord was telling me he is coming soon. This was the spring before Donald Trump was elected.

Donald Trump was getting ready to be elected.

Then God woke me up again. I did not date this at the time. But I was sleeping again, and in the morning right at the foot of my bed I heard an audible voice call out "Marty." I turned quickly. I thought who is in the room. Jesus was getting me up again. The voice was a kind voice, not aggressive at all. probably the Angel assigned to me carrying out Gods will.

Years ago I was entertaining a sin in my house before I was delivered of it. And as it was happening, an audible voice said with authority, "Stop sinning"!!! The voice was about six feet away.

I have not been sick since the 1990s, praise God. One of the reasons is because I know the source, the devil. So I rebuke him.

But in January of 2017 I got flu symptoms for the first time in all those years. I was alone in the house. So I rebuked the devil and his symptoms and quoted the healing scriptures over myself and then went to bed. As I was sleeping, my hand was sticking out and I felt a hand grab my hand. I looked up, and it was an angel standing at attention. I had peace and fell asleep again. When I woke up I was completely healed with no flu symptoms. Scripture for this is Psalm 91:9–12: Because you have made the Lord who is my refuge, even the most high your dwelling place, no evil shall befall you nor shall any plague come near your dwelling; for he shall give his angels charge over you, to keep you in all your ways. In their hands they shall bear you up lest you dash your foot against a stone.

I am glad to say that God has gotten to me now after all that. I am in the Word a lot and sometimes now I don't sleep all night because He is keeping me up and giving me understanding and open visions. Note that when God was waking me up, he never did it the same way twice. The three times he spoke were different words.

Other things that have happened at different times. I needed ten dollars for rent back in the earlier days when we didn't have much money. I seriously didn't know where I was going to get it and it was due the next day. I remember praying in the locker room, "God I need ten dollars for rent." I didnt want to borrow it. The shift wasn't over yet, and I had to go to the back of the plant for something.

I walked past a stack of pallets that were outside, and as I walked by, there was a ten-dollar bill pinched between two pallets flapping in the wind. I was taken aback. I prayed that prayer not more than two hours ago. Praise be to God. This was also a high traffic area where lots of people could have seen it.

I have been attacked three different occasions in my sleep by demons that I woke up and saw. One night I was on the couch sleeping, feeling pain on my right arm, and I woke me up. There were three demons standing there. Two were about the size of monkeys, and one was bigger about the size of a eight-year-old kid. I reached over with my left hand to grab one and as I did the demon squished through my fingers like Jell-O, and they all disappeared. No fear, just victory!

Then I was coming back from Wisconsin from a Mother's Day get-together heading back to Missouri. I had to stop at a parking lot to sleep for a while. We had a good meeting with family and spiritual progress was made with some family members. So as I was sleeping in the parking lot, my left arm hanging out towards the door, and I physically felt a biting pain on my hand. I woke up to see a rabid looking squirrel-type creature gnawing on my hand. There was pain but no damage. I reached over again, and it disappeared. Satan was furious at the spiritual progress being made with family.

These attacks that were coming from demons were coming because I was doing damage to his kingdom. Progressing in my walk with God. So the attacks were becoming external, manifesting in the natural. I was getting victories in my thought life especially in forgiving people; he couldn't get a root of bitterness in me. In other words, he wasn't succeeding in getting his thoughts in my mind to destroy me.

Jesus in me was getting the victories.

If you will do what Jesus says, Satan will have no legal right to you. He will fear you because of your authority in Christ!

Here is an example of the favor of God: One time in my life, I had a $15,000 interest debt I wasn't making progress on because the interest was so high but I was faithful to pay anyway. Suddenly God eliminated it. The company had no record of the debt.

On a thing like this, I was honest and doing my best to pay the debt, and God honored it.

Another time I needed to make a flight to New York from Kansas City with a layover at O'Hare in Chicago. This was for my son's military transfer of command ceremony. He really wanted me there, and I wanted to be there. I had very little time to get to the airport after work. My flight was at 9:50 a.m. I had a two-and-a-half hour drive to the airport from my house, then I had to find a parking spot in the United section. There was nothing, and time was ticking away. I said, God would you please give me a parking spot? Just then as I was moving, there was a spot! The only one left in the whole lot. I parked, I thanked God, and went running to the United terminal. Out of breath I had a half hour to spare, or so I thought! When I got to the United terminal they told me I was too late. They need a half hour just to load people on the plane, so the gate was shut. So I said "now what do I do?." The guy said wait and I will look.

Meanwhile I prayed, God please give me a flight and I thank you for it. The United employee took about ten to fifteen minutes locating a flight. I thought this was going to cost me a lot because it was my fault, even though it was the best I could do. The United guy said to me, this is very unusual!! I have never seen this before. I have an unscheduled flight that you can take in two-and-a-half hours, only you will be the only passenger on it.! I have never seen anything like this. I said "what?! This was a Boeing 737 jet all to myself. It was held over for repairs and was going back in service at O'Hare Airport. God made the arrangements. Thank you, God.

So I boarded the plane and the three flight attendants greeted me, saying they had never seen this before. Only one passenger! We had fun. They brought me a large water and snacks and the copilot came back to meet me. He said, I had to meet you. I have never seen a single paying customer on one airliner before. We took a bunch of selfies, but he wanted it for his own records. I am helicopter enthusiast and am looking to fly one someday. So as I was talking to the copilot, he said "do you want to see the cockpit? Yes I do!!! He put me in the captain's chair while he sat in the copilot seat. He was explaining to me the flight controls. Computer screens are used now. We had a great time. This was more than I could have hoped for. This copilot flew fighters in the Gulf War. I got all kinds of pictures with the flight attendants and the captain. God had taken a desperate situation and gave me more than I could have asked for. This is the favor of God you can have too. This did not cost me anything extra. I was told later it could have cost hundreds for rebooking because it was my fault.

I want to thank the United Airlines people for their treatment. The pilots and the flight attendants were great. I could see they all loved their work.

These testimonies are to encourage people that there is a living God who does care about you. He is no respecter of persons. What he will do for one he will do for another. But the change came for me when I received Christ in July of 1985. That's when the Supernatural Jesus started working in my life. Before that, he was keeping me alive and putting things in my path to bring me to a point to receive Him. I was going to a religious church since I was born for twenty-five years, but I did not know God and none of these supernatural things started happening until I received His Son Jesus in 1985.

My dad, being in his eighties, has been on death's door three different times in intensive care. Vitals were bad. The doctors wanted the last wishes recognized and asking about power of attorney. We would get into warfare prayer and healing prayer, and within hours he would come out of it. He lived three more years. He died of old age. He died of old age at eighty-three. God gave him 3 prophetic dreams all in one dream just before he died to get him to receive Christ.

His dreams were; He saw himself on a street. a crowd of people were going south and he was going the opposite way North, away from the people. In [Matthew 7:13,14] Jesus said, "Enter by the narrow gate; for wide is the gate and broad is the way is the way that leads to destruction, and there are many who go in by it. Because narrow is the gate and difficult the way which leads to life, and there are few who find it."

I believe my dad was being shown he will be taking the narrow path shortly opposite of the crowd. The thief on the cross got saved in his last hours of life.

The second part of the dream; He saw a priest walk into his room with a smile on his face and my dad knew that he was prostituting people. My dad was furious. He had always listened to them.

In the third part of the dream, a doctor came into his room smiling and he said he was prostituting nurses. my dad was really furious. These dreams bothered him. He had been around doctors and nurses for years because of his health issues. I believe that God was showing him some truth he might of been suspicious of in his life before he died. releasing him. This is not to imply somthing sexual.

Prostitute- [dictionary term] also means; Put one self or ones talents to an unworthy or corrupt use or purpose for the sake of personal or financial gain.

This is what my dad saw. My daughter and I sat with him in the hospital room two weeks before he died and gave him the gospel message. We believe he got in. He did not resist it this time.

You can do all the religious practices you want in any religion you want, but you really have nothing until you have Christ. Don't be deceived! Just because life goes on and their doesn't seem to be anything happening to you, and you're living a long and satisfied life and even growing old with a retirement plan. Thank God for that, but if you don't have Christ in your heart, born again, you're not going to heaven. Just doing what's right in your own eyes and paying God lip service does not mean He knows you. He knows you when He is in you. It's that simple.

If you live only by your conscience, just doing what you think is right all your life, the Bible says in Romans 2:14 that living like this, you are a law unto yourself. This means you declare your own righteousness. This is like filthy rags to God [Isaiah 64:6 and Romans 3:10]

Romans 2:12 says if you follow the law, the Ten Commandments, you will be judged by it. Either way, you will fail. The only righteousness God accepts is the blood of His Son as you believe and receive Him. Jesus is now the fulfillment of Moses law, so we go through Him to get to the Father. [LUKE 16:16]

Exercise your faith. Have favor with God. Be His child by deciding for God to be your Father. What good is being a father if your son or daughter don't want you as a father? You cannot ever enjoy them or have fellowship with them or trust them, and they will not hear your correction or receive your love. You have heard of parents rejecting kids, but it is also true that the kids can reject the parent. God did create you!! But you can still reject Him as your Father. God wants a heart relationship through His Son living in you.

I would like to end this chapter by saying that God has done far more in my life than can be written in this book, and more just recently. These are just some highlights. God has given me success, pulling me up from the poverty pit of life.

I have been a Maintenance Superintendant, Grounds keeper, Power House maitenance, TV station master control opperator, Cross country Semi truck driver and now a maintenance man over my own plant.

Who can measure what he does in a believer's life? He never left me or forsook me, and he will never leave you or forsake you if you will come to Him and continue in Him. Here are some other verses:

[JOHN 6:37] "All that the father gives me will come to me, and the one who comes to me I will by no means cast out.

[Matthew 7:22,23] "Many will say to me in that day, Lord, Lord have we not prophesied in your name and cast out demons in your name, and done many wonders in your name?" and then I will declare to them ' I never knew you; depart from me, you who practice lawlessness!'

These people in this parable were works-minded not repentance-minded. It was all about them. They praticed sin while ministering and Jesus at judgment didnt know them. Jesus will not abide sin. If you keep yours, you cannot have Jesus. He is Holy. Your heart is a throne to you, your body a temple. If Jesus is your Lord, He will kick out your sin once He gets into you on the throne of your heart. This is what Jesus was showing us when He turned over the tables and threw out the money changers. He was cleansing His Fathers temple.

In my own life when I recieved Jesus in 1985, The sin that didnt bother me for 25 years, as soon as I recieved Christ I started hating the sin that I used to enjoy, so it was not hard to give it to the Lord and let Him remove it from me. He replaced it with joy and righteousness. I could now start loving God and myself also. I liked the changes I was seeing in me.

Now the temple Jesus will cleanse is you. He will make you Holy in order for Him and His Father to dwell in you. Then you have eternal life. If you dont recieve Christ, somthing else is on the throne of your heart and it will not save you.

2 Timothy 2:19: Never the less the solid foundation of God stands, having this seal: the Lord knows those who are His; and let everyone who names the name of Christ depart from iniquity.

Matthew 7:24–25: "Therefore who ever hears these sayings of mine, and does them, I will liken him to a wise man who built his house on the rock: the rain descended, the floods came and the winds blew and beat on that house; and it did not fall, for it was founded on the rock." They gave their life to Christ.

[Matthew 7:26,27] "Now everyone who hears these sayings of mine and does not do them, will be a foolish man who built his house on the sand; and the rain descended and the floods came, and the winds blew and beat on that house; and it fell and great was its fall."

The house on the sand is the life built without Christ involved. Your way! The house on the rock is the life built with Jesus in your life and listening to Him.Internal strength. a built up Godly Spirit and renewed conscience.

A house's strength to withstand the weather and stress comes from the internal strength of the structure, not the beauty of the outside. We need internal foundational strength from Jesus to go through life righteously and get into heaven in the end. This is the house on the rock of Jesus. You will survive because he will help and strengthen you.

[ISAIAH 55:6,7] Seek the Lord while he may be found, call upon him while he is near, let the wicked forsake his way, and the unrighteous man his thoughts; let him turn to the Lord and he will have mercy on him.

You have faith!! God has given every man a measure of faith. [ROMANS 12:3]. It is up to you to decide to invest it into Jesus or invest it into something of the world.

There is a true story about a couple who wanted to adopt a child and went into a poor country orphanage to meet the kids. They talked with one of them that really melted their heart. They decided to file for adoption for him. Because of laws, they were not able to take him home yet. So this couple went back to the USA and waited, and sent a photo album to him, while they all waited. It was pictures of his new life. Where he would live, his bed room, his parents,etc. That boy held on to the album and showed every-body his new life he was headed for with excitment and anticipation.

The bible is a love letter to you and me. A photo album of the life that is ours. We should be excited and hold it in anticipation of our new life and our soon to be home in heaven. Read your bible. God backs up His own word. He will meet you where ever you are if you search for Him.

The saying is true: garbage in—garbage comes out! Good things in and good things will come out. Jesus and his word are the only good that will defeat the negativity of the world.

He loves you; receive Him. Here is a salvation prayer:

> Jesus. I ask you to come into my life, give me the new heart you promised, and wash my sins away and be my Lord and Savior, and I thank you for eternal life. Amen.

Thank you for reading this book. Looking forward to new brothers and sisters in Christ.

For whoever calls on the name of the Lord shall be saved. [ROMANS 10:13]